Kim Kuhteubl

BRANDING + INTERIOR DESIGN

Visibility and Business Strategy for Interior Designers

Schiffer Publishing Ltd.

4880 Lower Valley Road • Atglen, PA 19310

Designed by Shawna Armstrong
Cover design by Shawna Armstrong
Type set in Raleway/Arial

ISBN: 978-0-7643-5129-7
Printed in China

Published by Schiffer Publishing, Ltd.
4880 Lower Valley Road
Atglen, PA 19310
Phone: (610) 593-1777; Fax: (610) 593-2002
E-mail: Info@schifferbooks.com
Web: www.schifferbooks.com

For our complete selection of fine books on this and related subjects, please visit our website at www.schifferbooks.com. You may also write for a free catalog.

Schiffer Publishing's titles are available at special discounts for bulk purchases for sales promotions or premiums. Special editions, including personalized covers, corporate imprints, and excerpts, can be created in large quantities for special needs. For more information, contact the publisher.

We are always looking for people to write books on new and related subjects. If you have an idea for a book, please contact us at proposals@schifferbooks.com.

"[An interior designer] must be able to clarify his intent, keeping ever in mind that decorating is not a look, it's a point of view."

~ Albert Hadley

Inventory

Chapter 4: Clients That Fit   89

Chapter 5: Build Your Online Home   113

Chapter 6: The Power of Press 143

Chapter 7: Audience Building 101 167

Introduction

I've always had a thing for stripes—striped socks and pinstripes on jackets, especially—which is partly why bumblebees fascinate me. Add to this the fact that according to the law of aerodynamics, these bombini aren't structured to fly, and I'm in. Because that's the thing about bumblebees, they do fly.

In my conversations with designers, decorators, and architects, I hear a lot about being overwhelmed, bad clients, and cycles of feast and famine. Many have decided that consistent income is impossible to achieve, that they will never get published, or that they have to accept low-quality clients to earn a living. Yet all the while they cling to outdated business systems and beliefs. So let me clear this up: It is possible.

Scientists used to think bumblebees weren't structured to fly because they were comparing them to airplanes. But bumblebees don't fly like airplanes. Their wings create tiny, figure-eight hurricanes that generate enough force to keep them in the air. Even though it looks complicated, it's efficient, so much so that researchers mimic their mechanical structure in product design.

You may have been told that creative people aren't good at doing business. I think that's old "science." I believe they do it differently: from the inside out. The design process is a deeply personal one intertwined with emotion, values, and point of view. So to leave your personal interior planning—in other words, your emotional mastery—out of the process of building a design business is counterintuitive. To be leaders, designers must look not only at traditional measures of ROI, but also at intangible measures like quality of life, confidence, artistic challenge, and legacy if they are to build and sustain a thriving design practice.

Since founding my company Me By Design, I've worked with designers to increase their profitability, taking more than one client from six to seven figures in sales. I've helped them lay the foundation to create and negotiate product licenses and develop rosters of clients who are a fit for the way they work. I've seen them published in national shelter magazines like *Architectural Digest, House Beautiful*, and *Elle Decor*. I've helped them grow their teams, sell TV and digital series, and create opportunities for book deals and guest television appearances. These successes weren't flukes. They were claimed using a creative business blueprint I call a Visibility Strategy, one you'll learn about in this book.

You don't need to know how it's all going to come together at the moment. To be creative is to learn to navigate uncertainty. As Billy Baldwin famously put it, "A person with real flair is a gambler at heart." Whether it's a bedroom fluff or a whole-house renovation, if an idea that started out one way veers another way during the creative process, you roll with it. You get present, listen to your intuition, and improvise, taking inspired action until you figure it out, because you always do.

Why not try the same with your business? The solutions that will take it to the next level lie in your ability to master your relationship with the unknown. Navigating uncertainty requires vision, connection, confidence, patience, discovery, courage, expansion, and curiosity to achieve transformation. That's because no problem can be solved from the same level of consciousness that created it. Believe Einstein. He said it.

You don't know what you don't know, and not knowing what questions to ask is keeping you stuck and unseen. Now is the time for clarity. Decide that you will do what it takes to invest in your business and yourself in a way that allows you to soar. If you want to transform the results you're getting in your business, make the decision to start right now.

Take inspiration from the bumblebee. These busy little workers are built to fly, just like you're built to prosper. Ready for liftoff?

"When I draw up a set of plans there is no second choice. There is only what I show you. The best."
~ Elsie De Wolfe

The New Rules of Being Visible

1

In 1905, at age forty, Miss Elsie de Wolfe gave up acting for good and set up residence at the historic Washington Irving House in Gramercy Park, New York, with Miss Elizabeth Marbury, a prominent theatrical agent. The combination of de Wolfe's style and Marbury's connections transformed Irving House into the American version of a European salon. Issuing smart business cards embellished with a small wolf with a flower in its paw that would become her trademark, she started charging her famous friends to dispense her decorative savoir-faire. Hence, the profession of interior decoration as we know it, was born.[1]

Perfectly in tune with a small cultural revolution, de Wolfe quickly became known for her innovative and anti-Victorian interiors that espoused "plenty of optimism and white paint" and "suitability, suitability, suitability." A seasoned self-promoter, de Wolfe was a woman who knew her worth and was not afraid to charge for it. She sold Henry Clay Frick $3 million worth of furniture in fifteen minutes and collected a ten percent commission. She embraced publicity, became known for audacious behavior, and cultivated a lifestyle that her clients wanted to emulate, socializing with everyone and anyone who could afford her tastes. By 1912 she was America's "first lady of interior decoration." For the next fifty years, notable clients like Condé Nast, Paul-Louis Weiller, Cole Porter, and the duchess of Windsor earned her the reputation of the most famous decorator in the world.[2]

A smart business card, uncommon vision, and the right connections have launched more than one interior design career in the past 100 years, but in 2016, that's not enough to sustain it. Once shrouded in secrecy and the domain of an elite few, interior design has been catapulted into the public view via the internet. Even though traditionally, eighty percent of a successful interior designer's business was repeat business, our ever-changing online world gives a whole new urgency to the saying "out of sight, out of mind." DIY design, E-design, flash-sale sites, and online access to resources that were previously to-the-trade have changed the way the industry works, what consumers think they know about interior design, and what they're willing to pay for it. Today, the difference between surviving and thriving lies in one little word: brand.

Branding has come a long way from the days when ranchers coined the term to describe how they burned a symbol onto the skin of their herd to tell their animals apart. According to the American Marketing Association, a brand is defined as the "name, term, design, symbol, or any other feature that identifies one seller's good or service as distinct from those of other sellers." Consumers develop relationships with brands in a social, psychological, and anthropological sense, which is why big companies have long understood that a brand is the most valuable fixed asset of a corporation.

In the last decade, the personal brand (PB) has swung aggressively into focus as an essential component for designers who expect to stay in business for the long haul. Your PB, and by extension your firm, is what marks your services as distinct from other designers. It's the expression of your personality, values, aesthetic, and relationship with your clients. Whether it's the desire to feel successful, safe, at home, or like you've arrived, a legendary design brand is an emotional expression of universal human truths. When it's built and communicated in the right way, your essence or brand DNA makes you stand out in a crowded online market to capture the attention of your ideal clients.

A strong PB also undoes traditional notions of competition. Remember, there is only one you—even twins have different fingerprints—so if you confidently speak about yourself and your services from that singular place, you become inimitable in the marketplace. Sure, there will always be other people offering their design services, but none just like you and, depending on your audience, that singularity can command premium pricing.

Millennials, Millionaires & Mobile

If you're addicted to blaming the economy for your ebb and flow in sales, it's time to give that up: the economy is back. Despite the negative impact of the recession after the housing market collapse in 2008, the US remains the leading home goods market in the world—a $500 billion one.[3] Even in households with lower income, demand for home goods continues to grow as the housing market rebounds. However, recession in and of itself is not the most significant change to have impacted the design trade in the past decade.

"I've been in this business long enough to have been through four recessions," says Rosecrans (Crans) Baldwin, president of Dedar USA and director of Hermes Fabrics & Wallpapers. With more than twenty-five years of experience in all areas of interior furnishings, Baldwin is recognized as an industry thought leader and has helmed companies like Donghia, Bergamo, and a slew of design industry organizations. "One of the things I find fascinating is the rise and then fall and then rise of retail," says Baldwin. "The other big change, of course, is the rise of the internet, which has changed everything."

In fact there were eleven recessions between 1945 and 2001.[4] Unless you were very lucky or very connected, if you didn't adapt to the changes that started picking up speed around 2006, you probably went out of business when your pipeline of prospects emptied at the beginning of the most recent one.[5] Firms at the top of the marketing pyramid, however—those headed by designers with brand name recognition—returned revenues that were stable or grew. That's because their international clients in Russia, Dubai, China, and Europe were still buying.

Whether it's to purchase real estate or design services, the "one percent" is now a global group of people, and in recession-proof cities like London, New York, and Hong Kong, the internet has created an international "luxury" marketplace. However, the US still has the most millionaires, with roughly forty-four percent of the world's millionaire households. In fact, according to a study from the Boston Consulting Group, there's a millionaire living on nearly every block in America—one millionaire household for every sixteen households—or roughly 7.1 million households. [6]

"You can't just sit here and wish that the internet wasn't there," says Baldwin. "It's just changing . . . What we've had now is a recession combined with a major change in society and a generational change, all happening at the same time."

That major generational change is the rise of the millennials, or Generation Y, a group that at 80 million strong is the largest cohort size in history. In broad strokes, they were born between 1980 and 1999 and are known as a generation of connected, diverse collaborators. They're more tolerant of other races and groups than older generations, perhaps because eleven percent were born to at least one immigrant parent.[7] This big group has big buying power, not just by their own means, but also with the financial support of their baby boomer parents. They're also set to be the most educated generation in history, one that's changing the way institutions and associations deliver learning.

A wired world is the only kind of world that this optimistic—many call entitled—and socially minded group has ever known, and they like it that way. Technology, especially mobile technology, is their future, and because there are so many of them, it's ours. A millennial will probably use his cell phone to look for your services on Yelp, if not for himself, then for his baby boomer boss. Eighty percent of millennials sleep with their phone next to their bed.[8] They switch their attention between media platforms twenty-seven times per hour on average.[9] Not surprisingly, millennials are also the vocal, early adopters who put Facebook on the map and who have blown up the growth of Instagram and Pinterest in record time. They're reading reviews and exploring information on social networks because they trust recommendations from peers and friends more than from experts.

For "generation me," the personal brand is not seen as self-promotion, but as a means to identify passions and create a personalized path forward. What is a brand's stated mission and purpose? Is it compatible with their core values? In an economy where eighty-six percent of millennials are willing to share their brand preferences online[10], what could be a major opportunity for design professionals is often a disadvantage. Because when it comes to their website, social media, and email marketing, most designers don't know what their brand is, what their image conveys, or how to reach the audience who will pay for their services.

Even if the person you want to work with is close to retirement and you never want to do business in another state, let alone another country, you're not off the hook for mastering your online communication. Seventy-nine percent of Americans, or 244 million people, are spending an average of thirty-two hours per week online, especially on Facebook where the fastest growing demographic is women over 55.[11] By the way, these women control a net worth of $19 trillion and own more than three-fourths of the nation's financial wealth.[12] (Repeat after me, "Facebook business page!") By 2020, sixty-eight percent of the world's population will be online, and if you expect to be in business in the next decade, you must build a home there. Think of it this way: if even one percent of those new online consumers seek design services, that's over 47 million people. You only need a handful of these to run a six-figure business.

What Is a Visibility Strategy?

In a crowded online world, it's not always the most talented people who are noticed at first—it's the most visible. But being visible is about more than having a huge online following or getting published in a magazine. One of the most underused definitions of visible means to be available. The design leaders we all know—whom you may or may not love—weren't anointed design royalty by the chief designer in the sky. They started out like you. They honed their POV and created a sought-after experience that people are willing to pay for because it has emotional currency. Not only did they do what it takes to fulfill their vision, but they were available to receive it. They thought they could and they did.

Designers create not only a stunning visual picture inside of a space, but they also create a feeling as they read, shift, and transform the energy. If you know how to quantify this process and your aesthetic, your service can have a great deal of value. However, to be in business, you have to have clients, and designers are notorious for allowing their personal relationships with clients to impact the boundaries of their business ones. Learning to ask for your full value, manage your time and client expectations, and find work that is artistically challenging but that still pays the bills, is an inside job. It's a job that is equally as important in the brand-building process as your website, logo, and a geek to tweak your SEO.

Often, designers will say, *I need a really strong marketing strategy*. When I ask what they want to achieve with that strategy, the responses are usually excited and passionate. *I want bigger jobs! I want to get myself out there! I want to be seen!* I start by getting specific. What does "out there" mean and whom do you want to be seen by? Because there is no strategy without clear vision and success is measured in milestones. That's often when the passion and enthusiasm stops. What they are really asking me for is a plan that's not going to require them to do what it takes to get bigger jobs, get themselves out there, and be seen.

> *Newsletters don't work. I did a newsletter a couple of times,and it didn't work.*
> *I don't have time to do social media.*
> *I know this job is smaller than my minimum and is taking up a lot of time, but I'm going to get really great pictures and maybe referrals.*
> *This client isn't ideal, but I can manage him.*
> *I want to write a book someday, I'll worry about the blogging and social media stuff then.*
> *I'm too busy.*
> *I'm overwhelmed.*

It's ironic that the designers who are the most insistent on having a plan are usually the ones most resistant to following one. They want a plan that will not require any growth or expansion. They want a plan that doesn't include things they don't want to do.

Resistance is like sludge in the pipes, which means it often takes a shock of truth to get you back in flow. But that old saying about the truth is right: it hurts. Visibility Strategies are built on inspired action and change, so depending on how resistant you are to making those changes, you may find yourself shocked, often.

Strategies require intention. They involve making a decision to take the inspired action that will get you out there, working on bigger jobs and being visible. A Visibility Strategy is a conscious plan of action designed to ensure that the important parts of your business vision are seen. It fills in the cracks in your business foundation using emotional intelligence and mindset magic. It's your customized model for doing business from the inside out. Visibility strategies allow you to design your business and your life on your terms, because why bother otherwise?

Sounds like marketing right? Only if you get that marketing ain't what it used to be. The rules have changed. The internet has forced such concepts as transparent, organic, and authentic into the mainstream in a rapid sea change that has left no industry untouched, especially interior design. What it means to market has changed dramatically in the last decade—heck in the last year—and it will change again. And guess what? If you're looking for shortcuts, you're probably not in it to win it for the long haul. Because a really good Visibility Strategy, a plan made to fit your business, demands authenticity. It demands effort. It demands real and true communication that results in relationships built over time. It is not fixed and will evolve as you do.

A Visibility Strategy is not about putting on a front to get good PR. They highlight transparency in the way you do business. That means there is no one formula that works for everyone. Are there best practices? Sure. But the right Visibility Strategy communicates your unique POV, not only how you do business, but why. It allows you to confidently tell your story in the way that only you can, to the people who need to hear it the most. Although it focuses on concrete, actionable, and strategic business steps to increase your profits, passive income, and profile, it also takes into account the emotional experience you have in your business, that you must have creative growth, and that you want people to be affected when they experience your work.

A Visibility Strategy won't work if you're faking it. It's kind of like saying that you want to lose fifteen pounds eating cupcakes for breakfast, lunch, and dinner. (If you can make that work, let me know!) The strategy to unfold a vision will involve a lot of little actions, committed and strategic ones, pursued over time—in other words, baby steps. Interestingly, that's when they get a lot easier, when the unexpected happens to accelerate them, but not a second before.

"In order to change an existing program, you do not struggle to try and change the problematic model. You create a new model and make the old one obsolete."
—R. Buckminster Fuller

The right Visibility Strategy has transformed my business and my life. The work I've done on my blocks to being visible has unplugged what I thought I had to do and who I thought I had to be in order to feel successful. Like designers, producers use their creative vision to supply solutions to their clients. We come up with the right ideas and hire and manage the team that will bring them to life, tiptoeing around the sensitive egos laid like land mines along the way. I've been responsible for crews of up to thirty people, some working remotely; hired and fired staff; handled the budgets, cost reports, scheduling, execution, delivery, network deliverables, and marketing of projects with micro and major budgets.

I started working in production in 1997, and grew up in the film and television industry at a time when it was being rocked by change. Digital technology, the rise of non-linear editing, and Adobe Photoshop had disrupted everything, and suddenly everyone thought they could make a movie. It was true. The democratization that came with digital meant that it was finally cheap and relatively easy to tell a story, whether or not you were talented. I was part of the new wave and rose through the ranks, watching jobs that had been considered art forms—do you know what a negative cutter is?—become obsolete, along with those who refused to adapt.

In 2006, I moved to Los Angeles with a mission to take my career to the next level. Trouble was, I hadn't defined what that meant, so I ended up at ground zero. A lot of people call themselves producers in LA. Not only that, but many come from families of producers going back generations, and most of them are men. My experience in cable and lifestyle television, and my awards and international screening history as a filmmaker, didn't mean a whole lot because some people, without the experience I had, were better at selling themselves, or they had the right connections. But a girl's gotta eat, and I was determined to work my way in.

I watched and learned what I was supposed to do to fit into the system, but I couldn't shake the feeling that people were disposable, and I didn't like that. I learned to excel at handling difficult personalities, because usually I wasn't up for a fight or for looking like a bitch, and because as a freelancer, I wanted to make sure I kept working. Although it took a lot out of me emotionally, I didn't stick up for myself as often as I should have because I thought dealing with it was what I had to do to succeed. I also rarely asked for the full value of my services, because like most of the people I worked with, I was grateful to be working the insane hours expected so I could do what I loved to do. Even though I always felt broke and worried about where the next job was coming from, I didn't think there was another way. This was the business and I had to suck it up. I didn't know what I didn't know.

At the same time, the internet was changing the industry again. It was like the Wild West as YouTube, social media, and other online communication tools blew up the entertainment universe. Now everyone was calling themselves a producer, in spite of the fact that they didn't have professional credits and had never had to adhere to the standards of television production delivery, schedule, quality, you name it. Manage a budget? What budget? And yet they seemed to be leaders. Was I irked? Yup. Did it get way more competitive? You bet. But I didn't have time to complain if I intended to survive.

I knew that mine wasn't the only creative industry that was seeing seismic change. The music industry was the first creative industry to be turned on its head. Remember Napster? We've been given a play-by-play of the disruption in the two decades since then. The publishing industry faced similar challenges. Publishers and independent booksellers were competing with people who could self-publish titles without an imprint, agent, or anything but their laptops. Basically what I'm saying is that the business of being creative is different, more different than it has ever been, and it's not going to stop changing any time soon. So when it comes to understanding what's happening in the design industry, I get it. You are not alone.

As for me, I was tired of constantly looking for work so I decided I would do the responsible thing and take a full-time job at a network as an online news producer—a.k.a. wire copy rewriter. The position was below my skill set and not challenging creatively, but it was permanent. I submitted my application in early October 2010 and started the interview process around Thanksgiving. By the time I was hired, I'd gone through two sit-down interviews, a written test, and two phone calls to get the job. The last interview I had was in person with the director and the assignment editor to give me a tour of the studio, I had a sick, sick feeling in my stomach the whole time. I'd always trusted my intuition when it came to my storytelling, but when it came to life—in other words, my finances, not so much.

I looked around the dimly lit news floor, at the grim faces huddled side by side, and thought, "This isn't me." But I didn't know how I could be financially stable, save for retirement, and have benefits without a permanent job. I had to be realistic, I told myself, especially when it came to money. Which, in hindsight, is exactly why I didn't have any. "You'll get used to it," I told myself. I didn't. I never stopped hating it. Fifteen pounds and five months later I came to the end of the road, and after a lot of tears and anger and cursing myself for not being satisfied with a normal job like everyone else, I made what at the time seemed like a huge investment in a business coach. It was more money than I'd ever spent on myself for something like that, and logic told me that it was the stupidest thing I'd ever done. I was smart. I could figure things out. I was a regular DIY kind of gal. "You've been screwed," I thought, handing over my credit card. But there was also a tiny bit of excitement. This time, I paid attention.

In some languages, certain concepts or inanimate objects are considered feminine or masculine. When it comes to design, it's not uncommon to describe objects in terms of their masculine and feminine qualities. Those descriptions become more loaded, though, when they're applied to human beings. What does it mean to be feminine or masculine? Is gender a construct?

Many women have worked hard to take gender and the idea of femininity out of the conversation when it comes to career and to simply be recognized for their skills and talents, especially in architecture, a traditionally male-dominant field of design. I once heard a well-known California architect speak about a pivotal project that she completed post-divorce when she felt creatively expressed again. But she bristled when I asked if she considered that well-published home with curvaceous lines, one that brought her international acclaim, to be more feminine than her previous work. She pointedly said there was no difference between male and female. I get it.

As sometimes the only woman in the room, I would have never classified my POV or leadership style as feminine. That seemed like an old-fashioned notion, one I had absolutely no patience for. Add to this the fact that when tests of masculinity and femininity are given to creative people, they're more likely to identify with and exhibit the strengths not only of their own gender, but those of the other one, too. Creative girls are more dominant and tough than other girls, and creative boys are more sensitive and less aggressive than their male peers. [13] So why on earth would I qualify my ideas in a way that could remind my colleagues of my sex and risk limiting my opportunity?

After six months of working with my coach, though, I found that acknowledging and mastering qualities that are often more prevalent when women do business resulted in my increased prosperity and success. I learned that the framework for the way I live, produce, and lead is heavily R-directed. In terms of brain function, the left hemisphere handles logic, sequence, linearity, and analysis. The right handles rhythm, spatial awareness, color, imagination, emotional expression, context, and the big picture. Both sides of the brain work together. L-directed thinking is often qualified as masculine, while R-directed thinking is feminine.[14]

When it comes to doing business though, R-directed, feminine, thinking—more nonlinear, intuitive, and holistic—has been given short shrift. For some, even calling it feminine has a stigma, especially given that contemporary culture has associated so many trivial behaviors with femininity, like gossiping, acting emotionally crazy, and — ironically — decorating. However, when I stopped suppressing and devaluing the feminine aspects of my approach to business, I came to understand that it was like yin and yang, an equal, interconnected and necessary component of my winning business game.

By the end of that first year, I had almost doubled the salary I'd made at the network. I was doing business with clients I loved and in a holistic way that put the skills I most enjoyed using to full use. I now pay my own benefits and have the time and money to travel more than two weeks a year, and yes, I have a retirement portfolio. The best thing about it is that my Visibility Strategy doesn't have anything to do with what anyone else thinks is realistic, which is really only someone else's take on their experience. I have a new normal, and I am not alone. Over and over again, my clients have actualized their visions using Visibility Strategies crafted from the inside out.

Learning to Lead

Although I still firmly believe in the equality of men and women, I also acknowledge and celebrate the differences between them, equal but different. And even though both sexes tend to agree on the relative importance of top-tier leadership traits, there are documented differences between them. I also believe that in the context of leadership, femininity needs a makeover. This is especially relevant when it comes to interior design, because sixty-nine percent of interior designers—eighty percent unofficially—are women.[15]

It is difficult, if not impossible, to determine whether a piece of work was designed by a man or a woman. Where differences and distinctions often emerge is during the design process itself. Women apply a different psychological framework to decision-making in terms of establishing a design approach, interpreting the user's needs, and assigning priorities with regard to function or appearance. Men and women also differ in the way they make decisions and negotiate with team members.[16]

Dutch social psychologist and researcher Geert Hofstede describes as feminine those countries stressing equality, solidarity, work-life balance, and the resolution of conflicts by compromise and negotiation. According to a Pew Research Center study on women and leadership, although both men and women place importance on top-tier leadership traits like organization, decisiveness, honesty, and intelligence, women place more importance on the latter two. Women are also much more likely than men to say that being compassionate is absolutely essential in a leader. In fact, fully two-thirds of all adults say being compassionate describes women better than men.[17]

In his book *A Whole New Mind*, Daniel Pink refers to this heightened empathy, this ability to understand the subtleties of human interaction and to stretch beyond the norm in the pursuit of purpose and meaning, as "high touch." I can't think of a better way to describe designers' services. So we're going to emphasize this high-touch, feminine, and right-brained way of leadership and doing business in this book. Not only because it works but because in our digital age, this way of doing business has a high value. (If you're a creative man reading this book, or you're a woman who doesn't like the adjective, feel free to substitute R-directed as you read.)

The definition of good leadership is as diverse as the qualities and styles that define it. Although you may have been considered bossy as a child, depending on how you came to the profession, you may not think you are qualified to lead. There is an oft-talked-about glass ceiling that women hit in many industries, which is part of the reason they are more likely to leave and start their own business. But even for those interior designers who run their own firms, the power struggles can play themselves out with architects and contractors.

Women's leadership potential sometimes shows up in what have previously been considered less conventional ways, like being responsive to a clients' needs, for example, rather than asserting a point of view to get their own way. Dozens of studies have shown that women are generally better at reading facial expressions and at detecting lies. As early as age three, girls are better at inferring what others are thinking and at divining emotions from the expression on someone's face.[18] It's why some women are more likely to cry at another's distress. This unspoken communication between them, their clients, and their colleagues can affect how they lead and their willingness to be truly visible doing business.

As a leader, you must uphold a vision larger than yourself and the present moment. You must connect others to a larger purpose. You want your team to find deeper meaning in their work—all strengths of feminine leadership. But if you're introverted, as many creative women are, you may choose to do it quietly. Quiet leaders have additional challenges, especially when people with less vision and more volume keep demanding you pay attention to them. At some point as your firm grows, you won't be able to ignore what isn't being said. Whether it's firing a difficult client, not hiring them in the first place, calling out a vendor or colleague about their dishonesty, or asking for your true value in negotiations, this book will give you the tools to powerfully speak your truth and step into your vision. Leaders who speak with intention are a powerful force in the world.

How to Use This Book

In many chapters of this book, you will find a STYLESheet™ that you can work through to take your business to a higher level, whatever that means to you. The download arrows indicate that digital versions can be downloaded from the resource site www.brandinginteriordesign.com.

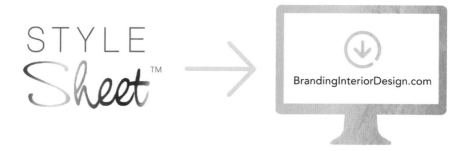

BrandingInteriorDesign.com

The headphones will let you know if there is anything extra to listen to at www.soundcloud.com/mebydesign.

Turn off your cell phone, completely. (If it's on vibrate, it's not off.) It's this kind of investment, focus, and determination that will help you create a custom Visibility Strategy. Go deep. Get real. Go for it. By that I mean answer every question and don't hold back. Whether it's a beach house, a seven-figure year, or a client that gives you carte blanche, write it down. There is something about the act of writing that will help your vision land in your body. If you can't answer a question right away, skip it and come back to it once you've completed the others. If something feels too big or impossible, write it down! Ignore the how-will-I-ever-get-that-done mind chatter for now.

Give yourself a solid chunk of uninterrupted time at the end of each chapter. Write out your top three takeaways and one action step that you can implement today. By the end of this book, you should have plenty of ideas to help you brand and market your interior design firm, and then some.

Are You Ready to Level Up?

Most of us have learned that it's not a good idea to burn bridges, because we think of that concept in terms of relationships. But what if we reframe it in terms of the unknown? Burn the bridges that keep you "safe," that keep you from diving in and running your business and your life with all of your energy. Once a bridge is broken, you can't swim back to shore. You have to make it to the other side. You have to reach your financial goals. You have to have amazing clients. You have to get published. Except try to remember that those have-to's are get-to-do's. Forget about business as usual. It's time to level up and design a business and life that brings you joy. So why not burn the bridge and leap to the other side? Let's go!

"I think it takes a long time not to have to prove to somebody that you're good."
~ Kelly Hoppen

Determine Your Brand DNA

The tiny city of Reims is one of my favorites in France. Reims played a prominent, ceremonial role in the story of French kings because its breathtaking, Gothic cathedral is where they were crowned. It's also home to the largest champagne houses in the world—les grandes marques—Vranken Pommery, G. H. Mumm, and Veuve Clicquot.

The houses are opulent and layered with stories as intricate and detailed as the process of making this sparkling liquid gold. Murano glass chandeliers hang in the maze of chalk caves 160 stairs below Jeanne-Alexandrine Pommery's former estate where the champagne is made and cooled. At Mumm's, one of the caves is as long as the Champs-Élysées and houses about 20 million bottles. Here also is a library of vintages dating to the 1800s. But it was the widow Madame Barbe-Nicole Clicquot who invented the racks all the houses use, where bottles are turned inch by inch, day by day, for at least four years until the sediment reaches the top and they're ready to drink.

The quality of champagne is determined not just by the nobility of the grape but also according to terroir, translated loosely as, "a sense of place." The unique aspects of a place—geography, climate, and terrain—influence and shape the flavor of the champagne made there. It's a beautiful metaphor for the design process. Designing a place is influenced by the geography of the space, the emotional climate of the people who will live there, and the wide-open terrain of your taste. It's about interpretation, and it's that interpretation, or your point of view, that is the essence of your personal brand.

That Thing You Do That Nobody Else Does

I start the brand decoding process with designers by asking the question: what's the one thing you do that other designers forget about? With a few exceptions, most will say:

I never forget the client!
I always include my client's personality in my design.
It's not about my style.
I'm designing for my clients, not me.
Sound familiar?

When I ask if that is their brand, most respond with a hesitant yes. But here's the thing. If everybody's saying that—and one look at the marketing and sales copy of many interior design firms shows they are—how does it distinguish you from the other designers offering their services? Yes, the profession's foundation is built on creating environments that reflect your client's personality, tastes, and needs. But consider this: what if your ideal clients came to you because of your terroir—in other words, because of your interpretation?

But I don't want to be known for one style!
I don't have a look.
I don't want somebody to look at a room I've designed
and know it was designed by me.
I'm versatile and will not be boxed in!
If I get known for doing one thing, I'm going to limit the
number of clients I can get.

Do you think Barbara Barry, whom you'll hear from later in this book, worries about being known for her singular look? Or that Vicente Wolf is trying desperately to climb out of his box?

You don't have to have a "look" to become a well-known brand, but you must have a POV. Take Martyn Lawrence Bullard as an example— you'll hear from him in chapter 7. Whether it's an Italian castle, the homes of the Hilfigers or a Russian oligarch, you would expect someone as bold and creatively fearless as Bullard to be a fit for his high-profile clientele. In our increasingly electronic world, where it's sometimes difficult to discern if what we see is real or manufactured, people that are perceived as authentic, transparent, and true become leaders in their field. Their brands become synonymous with trust. Because we all want to do business with people we can trust.

The most successful designers are known for being, and revealing, themselves. Being yourself is timeless. It's a universal experience, something we are all capable of doing, even though we all do it differently. Your clients may not have a design vocabulary. They may not know how to express or achieve your style, but they hire you because they resonate with something visually and, most important, emotionally when they look at your portfolio. Although your job is to interpret their personality and transform the way they see themselves, it happens through your very specific visual lens. The value of your brand happens in your interpretation. Because while you can't bottle your client's precious found objects and vacation photos, you can capture the emotional essence of your aesthetic, that design thing you do, and turn it into a scalable and profitable business.

Not to mention the fact that the whole point of having a personal brand is that it's personal. When it comes to design and lifestyle brands, the most memorable become known because they are about aspiration and inspiration. People want to live the life they see designers creating and living. Is your lifestyle on-purpose and inspired? Or are you in business just to pay your bills? Designers who take what they truly desire out of their business equation are effectively taking themselves out of business.

Your value lies in the experience you offer clients and the expectation of what it can do in their lives, and it increases only as much as your perceived value to your audience. Think about it: the higher a person's income, the more she is being paid for who she is, rather than for what she does or sells. Sure, there are plenty of television hosts, but only one Oprah. When it's Ralph Pucci, TOTO, Phyllis Morris or La Cornue, buyers aren't haggling for price. They're buying not just for practical reasons, but also for ego and emotional reasons. It's a delicate equation and your worth and your client's estimation of your worth must be a match if you're going to do business.

Whether you're offering luxury goods or not, the same can apply to you. What's more emotional than designing a home and helping the people who live in it express themselves fully with comfort and ease? Home is where we spend most of our time, love our families, and make memories. Once you've established a design brand worth buying, you won't have to prove the value of your fee to your clients. Your clients will be set on working with you and only you, and willing to pay for that experience.

So how do you define your brand's DNA—what your business is made of—and quantify that thing you do that clients want to buy? When I worked as a freelance story producer covering real estate, development, and design, I was always chasing guests to book for segments. For TV, tight deadlines and last-minute cancellations meant that sometimes I had to find someone to come into the studio in a matter of hours. After experiencing a couple of awkward interviews, I quickly figured out the type of person who was going to deliver. Without exception, the people who were compelling guests had mastered three communication qualities:

Clear Vision   A Unique Story   Energy   Your Brand DNA

Working with interior designers on their branding, I've noticed this same equation holds true. If any one of these elements is missing, either online or when we speak in person, the imbalance causes a disconnect.

Here are a few of the most common ways connection is lost in a designer's online marketing:

- You have a high-touch residential firm that requires a high-level of intimacy, but you don't have a photo of yourself on your biography page.
- Your marketing copy emphasizes quality, but you don't have a professionally photographed portfolio.
- Interior design is your second career, and yet your biography boasts all the accomplishments of your first one.
- You list all the services your company offers, kind of like listing   all the parts of a Mercedes, expecting your

audience will understand how they fit together, rather than describing your overall process.

- You list the details of a few packages, usually the most "affordable" ones, and then wonder why nobody hires you for the full-gut renovations with large budgets that you want to do.
- Your entire website, or tabs like "products" or "blog," are under construction, and they have been for some time. Remember, clients are hiring you for your ability to manage and deliver their project. Why aren't you delivering for yourself?

Download case study examples at BrandingInteriorDesign.com.

"True originality consists not in a new manner but in a new vision."
~ Edith Wharton

Clear Vision

You need a blueprint to build a building; the same goes for your business. Leaders create a vision for themselves beyond where they are now. Your vision is the blueprint for both your creative expression and the way you want to live. As a creative person, the life you live and the way you express yourself are deeply intertwined. What you see is what you sell, and what you see will be affected by the experiences you have and your ability to receive an expanded capacity for living.

Whether you want a handful of six-figure jobs per year, to have a line of fabrics based on your illustrations sold nationally, or to be on the

AD100, your vision creates a plan of action for you and your team to follow: now. If your vision is muddled, you're likely making a mess taking every project, no matter how difficult the client or whether it's challenging you. When you're focused on what you want and where you're going, and it's in alignment with your values, what you're willing to offer in exchange becomes clear. Your vision sets the standard that determines your course of action now. As an entrepreneur you will assume all the risk and all the reward, and it's much easier to roll with it if you're starting from a vision set with intention.

Take your business to a higher level by asking yourself why you are in business. In his widely popular TED talk "How Great Leaders Inspire Action," author Simon Sinek says that legendary companies inspire action by communicating from the inside out.[2] Think about Apple, a company with rabid fans and brand ubiquity. Did you know it has only 7.5 percent computer market share?[3] Companies like Disney and Virgin also have ubiquitous brand recognition even though they own fractions of the markets they sell products in. They don't talk as much about what they sell—computers, entertainment, or airline services—they talk about why they sell them and what is possible in the lives of the people who use them. They are known because of the values, personality, and lifestyle associated with them. A list of your design services like space planning, design concepts, procurement, and installation is the what of your service, but if you want to be memorable, you must sell the why.

Your why is born of your values—your standards of behavior as a human being. It's bigger than you. When your business is a reflection of your core values and rooted in who you are, it is much easier to invest the time, energy and money required to navigate the twists and turns of running it. How do you want to be in service in the world? Who are you going to serve and how? What problem do you see over and over that you want to find a solution for? What are you doing to improve your craft? What one creative challenge have you set for yourself this year?

When Elsie de Wolfe started out, the need for her services was unknown, so she set out to create it. Although wealthy Americans were traveling to Europe in search of art and antiques for their collections, they usually relied on dealers to handle transactions, and those dealers certainly weren't women. De Wolfe believed that "a person's environment will speak for their life, whether they like it or not." But she also worked doggedly for women's suffrage. When her book, *The House in Good Taste*, was published, de Wolf proved that a woman who wanted to work, or had to, could excel without damaging their reputation.[4] How incredible then that over a century later, the profession she created is one in which the majority are women.

Her decoration, which looks tame by today's standards, either broke all the rules or established rules where there were none. She introduced humble glazed cotton chintz—once thought suitable only for slipcovers in country homes—into formal settings. She established interior design standards by giving people what they needed instead of what they wanted, and she had an uncanny ability to convince them that she was the final authority on matters of taste.[5]

Known for her English country look, Sister Parish was the first interior designer brought in to decorate the Kennedy White House. She went to work because her husband Harry's business and her father's business had fallen on hard times during the Depression. A woman "who had never opened a window or poured a glass of water myself," she was accustomed to living a certain way and was going to do everything in her power to maintain it for herself and her children. At age twenty-three she opened her decorating business in a small shop in Far Hills, New Jersey, and worked for the rest of her life.[6]

Sister Parish was credited with inventing the "American country" look, which sprang from a love of her parents' country house in Maine. Her "Yankee roots" were an integral part of her personality. She took immense pride in the fact that her American ancestors, Cotton Mather and Oliver Wolcott, signed the Declaration of Independence.[7]

The first time I read about Ruby Ross Wood, it was in a footnote. Wood, whose pen name was Ruby Ross Goodnow, was the ghostwriter of Elsie de Wolfe's famous decorating manual, *The House in Good Taste*. In fact, she was the first lady in decoration's voice in print for many years before that. Wood is part of the reason that Elsie de Wolfe became so famous. Wood also wrote her own book, *The Honest House*, and founded a design firm that flopped, but got a big break in the 1920s when she became manager of Wanamaker's Au Quatrième, the queen of department store decorating shops. She founded the first department store decorating salon. It's how Billy Baldwin found her.[8]

Billy Baldwin was considered the greatest influence on a generation of post-WWII designers—hence his nickname "dean of interior decorators." He studied architecture at Princeton but dropped out after two years and went on to decorate the homes of Jacqueline Kennedy Onassis, William S. Paly, Cole Porter, and Diana Vreeland among others.[9] Billy spent thirteen years being mentored by Wood, calling her "quite simply the finest decorator who ever lived."[10]

Popular among her New York circle of peers, if not among glitterati clients, Wood was seen as a new breed of female designer. She wasn't a socialite. Her family, although well-off, was not considered rich. She was said to be sharp-tongued and impatient, a "working" girl. She was opinionated about what worked and didn't work in a room. Once, she decorated her Manhattan drawing room entirely in molten vermilion—walls, lampshades, rug, ceiling, curtains, and upholstery.[11]

I am grateful to Wood, not because I had to look up vermilion and now have that acid color scorched onto my brain, but because she so beautifully illustrates that a creative life is often a circuitous one, and that the threads of connection that creativity weaves are miraculous, usually unseen, and often lasting. Sandwiched between two legends, she managed to become an integral part of design history simply by expressing her arts. "You cannot see actual growth, but you discover by looking back from day to day and from year to year that there has been growth," she wrote in *The Honest House.* "You find yourself in a room that yesterday seemed unobjectionable, and today you resent its ugliness. You look at a vase that you once thought beautiful, and realize that it is impossible. When you know that the room is ugly and the vase is impossible, ask yourself why it once appealed to you, why it now offends you, and if you can answer you have traveled far toward good taste."[12]

Now go back and re-read that passage, substituting the word "website" for room and "brand" for vase. What have you created? Is your online home a true reflection of your business vision and aesthetic, now? Does it tell the story of your brand DNA, of where you are today? Who do you think you're connecting with? Do you think you'll be a footnote, a leader, or a legend? Will it matter?

"Be faithful to your own taste because nothing you really like is ever out of style."
—Billy Baldwin

Permission Granted

You may not know what it is you really want, which is why you're overwhelmed or burnt out, being dragged along by the momentum of being an entrepreneur. A lack of clarity around vision is most often related to permission. (Indecision and fear are involved, too, but we'll talk more about them in the next chapter.) Have you given yourself permission to want what you truly want, whether it's a six-figure income or a house on the beach? Or are you making yourself wrong for the things you desire? Or have you stopped dreaming because you're worried about how much it's going to cost?

Asking for more can be especially uncomfortable if you don't feel like you have enough now, or if you've asked for more before and it didn't work. But here's the thing: if you don't ask, you don't get. I know you have no problem asking for more for your family, your clients, or for anyone else who is lucky enough to be in your care. But there is a reason that in a flight emergency, you have to put your own mask on first.

Start by writing down the things you love doing, even if they're not related to your business. Don't listen to the voice that tells you, "I can't make any money from that." Or the one that asks you how you're going to pay for it. Getting stuck in the hows will always interrupt the flow of your vision. If some part of you thinks it's impossible, it will be.

Your desires are as individual and perfect as your fingerprints. Why would you have the desire in the first place if some part of you didn't know that you could achieve it? Remember, too, that your personal expansion and business expansion are interconnected. Yes you want more clients and to make more money, but why? Do you want to travel to Morocco or Italy? Do you want to improve your health care or beauty regimen? Do you want time to redesign your kitchen or add a second floor to your home? When you feel good, you are renewing creativity, and that fresh point of view will make its way into your work.

"I have been accused of being dogmatic. I am. I would be useless to my clients if I were not, and if I did not have strong personal ideas on taste and design I would not be any good at doing my job. But I try to remain an interpreter of my clients' ideas and only become dictatorial when I feel they are making a mistake."
—David Hicks

 VISION

Right now your job is to dream. Dream big. Ask yourself what you really—I mean really—want. Do your business goals support your lifestyle goals, and vice versa? Play the whole tape through. For example, if you value your privacy above all else, you probably won't enjoy the visibility and audience engagement that having a popular television show demands. If your kids are little, you may want to keep your client load small. Remember, this doesn't have to be forever. However, getting clear on what you really, really want in the next six to eighteen months will direct the course of action you take now.

1. What is your why?

2. If you could be known for any one thing as a designer, what would that be? Remember, it doesn't have to be a look.

3. What three adjectives describe your design POV?

4. Consider that in five years, your design practice is wildly successful. Describe it in as much detail as possible.

5. What core values do you want your business to embody?

6. What does your perfect average day look and feel like?

7. Who are the people who surround you and support you?

8. How are you stretching yourself creatively?

9. Where have you traveled?

10. What do you do for me-time?

I've long loved the Beverly Hills Hotel, the iconic pink stucco hotel and bungalows at the foot of the Santa Monica mountains on Sunset Boulevard. But I didn't know that "The Pink Lady" was built by Margaret J. Anderson in 1912, before there was even a city called Beverly Hills. Hoping to ignite a land rush, the Rodeo Land and Water Company hired Anderson and her son to build a sprawling hotel in mission revival style on twelve acres. On opening invitations, Anderson described the property as situated "halfway between Los Angeles and the sea," and by 1914, Beverly Hills had attracted enough residents, including Mary Pickford and Douglas Fairbanks, to incorporate as a city. It became one of the world's smartest addresses.[13]

The story of this iconic landmark's first architect, Elmer Grey, and the current foreign royal owner is well known. But the story of the building's first interior designer—an equally important piece of its legacy—has fallen off the page. An artist's work usually survives beyond their lifetime, but not so with the creations of interior decorators. Buildings are razed and residents come and go. Even historical preservation societies concentrate on architecture rather than interiors. Why? Is it because designers don't like to tell their stories? Is it because they don't have the confidence to claim their work?

Stories are about connection. They teach, persuade, inspire, and even heal. Your story is built into every cell of your experience and offers credibility; it is your choice whether it will remain untold. Like everything else, your story will cause people to love you, want to get to know you, trust you, or dislike you, but no matter what, it can't be taken away from you. By telling a story, you plant ideas, thoughts, and emotions into your audience's mind. The way you tell your own story is exclusive to you, and the role of the language you use is the agreement you've made with your situation, now.

As a writer, I'm biased to believe that words are powerful magic. As a matter of fact, the word abracadabra may derive from an Aramaic phrase meaning "I create as I speak." In Hebrew, the phrase translates more accurately as "it came to pass as it was spoken." Tell the story of who you are and where you've been, but if you want to take your business to the next level, start telling the story of where you'd like your firm to grow. For example, if you are known locally, start talking about the fact that you are available to do work nationally.

The stories of design legends are as individual as their aesthetic. Beauty is subjective, but your taste, attitudes, belief system, travels, and experiences—all the defining qualities of your POV—are not. The right story about you and your experience will be attractive to your audience of clients who fit because in revealing yourself authentically, you provide an opportunity for them to connect with you.

Shortly after her forty-second birthday, another broken marriage, and scandal, fate was finally kind to Syrie Maugham. She credits her daughter as the creative impetus for her decorating career. "I began it all in Liza's nursery when she was a baby girl. I had plenty of time on my hands and I just began to play about with colors and designs for the house."[14] When her friend was about to throw away a large group of fluted wrought iron garden furniture, she rubbed it down, painted it white, and sold it for a huge profit. Other small jobs followed, and eventually she opened a small shop at 85 Baker Street in London, getting the bulk of her inventory and capital from the sale of her home, along with small loans from friends.

Her friend Elsie de Wolfe said, "You're much too late, my dear. Much too late. The decorating field is already overcrowded."[15]

But Maugham had just arrived. In 1927, she presented her all-white room at a midnight party at 213 King's Road for the most fashionable and stylish guests of the day. Harper's Bazaar devoted an article to her house, describing the music room as having white walls, white satin slipcovers, white velvet lampshades, and a pair of white porcelain camellia trees four feet high. The dining room's pine paneling had been striped and waxed, providing a background for rock-crystal-white painted chairs.[16] She even went to the extreme of having her living room canvas draperies dipped in white cement and filled the room with massive flower arrangement of all-white flowers: lilies, stock, gardenias, and chrysanthemums. It was a totally impractical design, yet theatrical. That night, Maugham became known as the White Lady. By 1930 she had design shops in London, Chicago, and New York, and her style was copied everywhere, including on the Hollywood screen in Jean Harlow's boudoir.[17]

Maugham had a flair for decorating, but her real genius was her ability to market her designs. She used every social contact and social encounter, especially her infamous dinner parties, to create a glamorous mystique around her profession. She did not invent the all-white room, but she was the first person to market this idea so successfully that it became her signature. Where others just used white, Syrie used parchment, ivory, oyster, and pearl.

"If she bought a thing from us for, say, seventy pounds, she'd probably charge seven hundred for it," wrote Victor Afia who worked with her in the early 1920s. "But she was clever, she knew that she could get away with it. After all, it wasn't the stuff so much as her talent she was charging for . . ."[18]

And the moral of the story? Ignore the noise and opinions of those who tell you it can't be done. Push your creative vision to the edge. Risk boldly. Charge appropriately.

Now I'm not suggesting you add the story of your messy personal life to your business bio—although depending on who you're targeting, that could definitely be a connection point in an in-person meeting. However, you can start telling the story of what you do in the way only you can. The right story about you and your experience will resonate with your audience—that is, if you know who you're talking to. More on that in chapter 4.

What is your story, and how do you want it to be told? Be specific about your background, how and where you studied design, and your process. If minimalism is your thing, say that. If being raised in the South shaped your values around home, say that. Choose your words carefully, whether using adjectives like historic, legacy, iconic, chic, midcentury, modern, or traditional. Use the answers to the questions below to isolate the details you will use in telling the story of who you are, where you've been, and where you want your firm to grow.

1. Are you an interior designer, decorator, stylist? What do you call yourself?

2. Do you specialize in residential, commercial, contract, hospitality, health care, universal design?

3. Where were you born? Raised?

4. Have you won any awards?

5. Where did you study? Do you have any certifications like LEED, CAPS, etc.?

6. Where have you traveled? Have your travels influenced your POV?

7. Any significant moments in your career you want to highlight? How about creative influences?

8. What professional associations do you belong to? Are you involved in charitable work?

9. Does the current city you live in influence your work?

10. What is your process? What are three defining characteristics? Which is the most unique?

11. What geographical areas do you serve?

"Never forget that you are one of a kind.
Never forget that if there weren't any
need for you in all your uniqueness to
be on this earth, you wouldn't be
here in the first place."
—R. Buckminster Fuller

Just like in conversation, depending on who your audience is, the way you tell your story will change. Although copy like "we put our clients needs first" sounds like good marketing, it assumes your client knows how to define what their needs are. What if the person reading has never worked with a designer? What if to serve them you must offer services outside the scope of what they think they need? Nor does that kind of general marketing speak explain your why.

As a prospective client, how can I trust that you will deliver if I don't have a context for who you are as a human being? Are the people who hire your firm corporate professionals or stay-at-home moms? Are you targeting residential or corporate clients? Have they worked with a designer before? Should the copy be more emotional and casual or will it be a formal bio written in the third person? Also, is your written story congruent with the style of the visual story told in your portfolio?

We will work on your ideal client extensively in chapter 4, but for the next exercise, consider how your answers to questions in part 1 change if you imagine your ideal client standing in front of you. Will the details you reveal change? Hint: they should.

1. Based on your answers in part 1, is there anything your ideal client would find more or less interesting?

2. Has your ideal client ever worked with an interior designer?

3. Is your written story congruent with the online visual story you tell in your portfolio?

4. What details are missing from the story you've told about your process that your ideal client would ask you in an interview?

5. What funny anecdote or memory would your ideal client appreciate? It may be something you've already shared in conversation as you work together.

Energy

The last piece of the brand DNA puzzle is the least tangible and most important. Energy is a dynamic quality, our usable power. It's the fundamental entity of nature, transferred between parts of our systems, and the building blocks of all that is. Not to bore you with physics, but what it boils down to is this: everything is energy and energy is everything. In terms of your PB, energy is about resonance. Resonance is the current running through the heart of your brand. It is the richness or significance and the associations that your brand and brand experience creates with your audience.

What is the quality of your work, and of working with you, that makes it personally meaningful to someone else? What is the emotional experience that people get when they walk into one of your rooms or see them captured in photographs? Your clients' response to who you are is an instant, unconscious impression that affects how they respond to you. Are you laid back, prickly and sarcastic, or quiet and thoughtful? None of these personality traits is more desirable than any other except to your ideal client. Then it's these traits that make you a match. It's why clients resonate with you, why they hire you instead of somebody else, and why working with you makes them feel like they've come home.

A study by researcher Albert Mehrabian found that non-verbal cues represent fifty-five percent of our communication when we are face to face. Vocal inflection is just thirty-eight percent, and our words constitute only seven percent of our communication. Hence the saying that actions speak louder than words. Because even the most subtle physical cues— from how you have your hands placed to how you hold your shoulders— set a tone. The energy of your marketing materials, photography, written copy, what you wear to a client's home for that first meeting, must reflect not just who you say you are but who they feel you are. Your energy is contributing to your relationships with others whether you like it or not. When your energy is off, people can feel it. They will unconsciously disconnect from you and your offer, and they won't know why.

Ultimately, energy directly impacts the visibility and long-term success of your business. If you're doing everything right and your business still isn't in the place where you'd like it to be, it's almost always about energy.

In the next chapter, we'll look at how energy, emotion, and mindset are woven together and how what interior designers think about themselves and their business directly impacts their ability to attract high-level clients, recognition, and above-average profit.

"The essence of interior design will always be about people and how they live. It is about the realities of what makes for an attractive, civilized, meaningful environment, not about fashion or what's in or what's out. This is not an easy job."
~ Albert Hadley

 ENERGY

Aristotle said the energy of the mind is the essence of life. Answer the following questions about your energy. Use the STYLESheet™ to figure out how you want your PB to make people feel.

1. What three qualities would you use to describe yourself?

2. What words have three people you admire used to describe you?

3. Do you agree or disagree with their description?

4. What words have people who aren't your fans used to describe you (that you know of!)?

5. Do you agree or disagree with their description?

6. How do you want people to feel during the process of working with your firm?

```



```

7. From an aesthetic standpoint, what is the emotional essence of your brand?

```



```

8. Are you easily influenced by the opinions of your peers?

```



```

9. When you spiral into negativity or complaints, what are you talking about? Thinking about? Do they correspond?

```



```

10. On a gut level, are your marketing materials congruent with the emotional essence of your brand?

```



```

The Hoppen Bubble

Designers can learn a lot about branding from leaders at the top of the marketing pyramid. Kelly Hoppen is one of those leaders. Her ever-evolving style is underpinned by a subtle coordinated fusion of East meets West—clean lines and neutral tones, blended with charming warmth and sumptuous opulence. She puts her stamp on the homes, yachts, and jets of private clients as well as select commercial projects the world over, including hotels, bars, restaurants, offices, and aircraft.

With forty years of experience at the forefront of the industry, publishers and businesses continually seek Hoppen's unparalleled expertise, allowing her to indulge her entrepreneurial instincts. Because she is passionate about making her design ethos accessible to the masses, Hoppen launched her eighth book, *Design Masterclass*, in November 2013.

@MEBYDESIGNTV:

Your business has a lot of different elements—design, licensing, television, publishing. Was that planned? And did you think you would be a success?

I'm often asked whether I thought I would be as successful as I am, and the answer is yes. I mentor a lot of young entrepreneurs, and you can sense when somebody has that ability to be successful in business. I think it's a quality you're born with, and my parents were very much a part of that in the way I was brought up.

My passion drove my business, and ultimately my passion is designing. When you think about a business, it's like a mind map, and from that one philosophy you grow and grow. So I was lucky that somebody saw that I was a designer who could become a brand.

I started to design products for other people to enhance their businesses, and the business grew quickly. Then, obviously, publishing allowed millions of people to see my work. When I first started writing, it was quite rare to find interior design books. So I guess I started at the very beginning.

@MEBYDESIGNTV:

What is the essence of your brand?

@KELLYHOPPEN:

I describe myself as a purist, because I'm not a minimalist at all. I'm a purist in that I have defined the art of living in a space that feels very Zen and harmonious. I'm a designer who defines a space by the people who live in it. I'm a designer who defines the space so that your art can speak in a room. I'm a designer who creates layers of texture, whether it's lighting, which I describe as a texture; fabrics; stone; wall colors; the way sound feels in a space; or the way food smells in a kitchen. It's all about finding balance in a home, and that is very important to me. It's about sensual interiors, because it's all about the senses.

@MEBYDESIGNTV:

Do you like the word brand?

@KELLYHOPPEN:

It's not my favorite word, but it's how we are defined today. We follow brands. We're obsessed with brands. We've created a world that follows celebrity endorsements. I know I'm a brand, and I'm proud of what I've

Right: Interior design by Kelly Hoppen. Photo by Mel Yates

created, but it's more of a style counsel, if you like, in that people will go and shop for a piece of clothing because they believe in that brand.

A brand only works if its philosophy is authentic. If I look back at the first interview I ever did, I see that my philosophies haven't changed. Now, if you ask me who I admire in the world of fashion and design, my first answer is always Ralph Lauren. He put that stick in the ground, "This is my brand philosophy." And he's never, ever changed it. Donna Karan's another one. It's quite rare with interior designers, but fashion designers have actually mastered it. When you look at an advert without a name under it and you know whose it is, that is a pure brand. People can say, "That's very Kelly Hoppen," and that's probably what I'm most proud of, rather than it being just a brand.

@MEBYDESIGNTV:
What is your philosophy on service, and how do you use it to differentiate yourself in the marketplace?

@KELLYHOPPEN:
Service has to be number one. People know that if we say they will move in next Tuesday, they're going to move in next Tuesday. When we say, "This is what it's going to cost," and they sign off on a budget, we give them the job for that amount of money. I think service is about taking away the pain, because it is painful enough to design and build a house without worrying about whether the person on the other end of the phone will deliver what they said they were going to deliver.

There are many designers out there that have a massive ego. I certainly did when I started forty years ago. I soon realized that you can't have one, that you're being paid to provide a service, whether or not that service incorporates the fact that you're a genius. You're providing a service the same way a plumber does when he fixes your pipes, so you have to provide it on time, within budget, and beautifully. At Kelly Hoppen Interiors, that's what we do, and we're renowned for it.

@MEBYDESIGNTV:
What one thing has been critical to building your company's long-term success?

Right: Interior design by Kelly Hoppen. Photo by Mel Yates

@KELLYHOPPEN:

Undoubtedly, it's communication. We call it the Hoppen bubble. If I'm in my studio on a Monday morning, I get everyone in and talk to them. Some of my staff members have been with me fifteen years. They've learned the way we work. We make sure that we're always ahead of ourselves, that we're always stepping outside the box and looking back in to see how we can better it, because the competition is out there. But one thing we never try to do is change who we are. We know who we are as a brand. So it's about communication within your company, and communicating authentically to your clients about what you can and can't deliver.

@MEBYDESIGNTV:

Is there anything you would have done differently?

@KELLYHOPPEN:

I don't think so. I never have regrets in life because you grow faster and bigger through your mistakes. I say to the kids I mentor, "Don't be frightened of making mistakes, because you will." I think intuition has been my biggest trump card. Women have amazing intuition, and if I follow my gut, I never go wrong.

Follow Kelly Hoppen, on Instagram, Twitter, Facebook, and Pinterest: @KellyHoppen. To watch selections of this interview on video visit www. youtube.com/mebydesigntv.

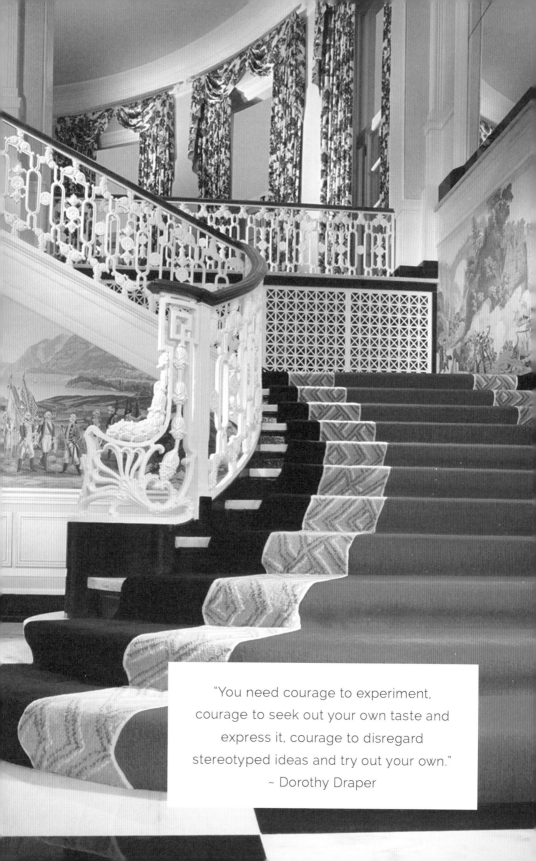

"You need courage to experiment, courage to seek out your own taste and express it, courage to disregard stereotyped ideas and try out your own."
~ Dorothy Draper

Interior Planning

In meteorology, visibility is a measure of the distance at which an object or light can be clearly perceived. Apparent, obvious, and seen are other synonyms. In this chapter, consider one of its underused definitions: available. Whether it's for high-profile press opportunities, a massive online following, a six-figure payday, or to be recognized with an award, ask yourself if you are truly available to receive what you've asked for.

The difference between unknowns, design leaders, and legends is a factor of the quotient of visibility. That measure will dramatically impact the expression, value, and longevity of your brand's DNA. Many designers stop short of success because they don't get that the art of being visible is an inside job. Disconnects between being, doing, speaking, and receiving all have underlying emotional roots that will impact your business growth. I call them visibility issues.

I know. You've got your reasons for hiding out. Designing the place where someone is going to live is emotional business. You juggle multiple personas—artist, therapist, negotiator, mediator, salesperson—and it can be tricky to navigate the expectations that come with each role. But if you don't trust the judgment of the person looking back at you in the mirror, how can you expect your clients to? That is, if you've even managed to attract clients who respect the value of your services in the first place.

Noise. From the newspaper, to your peers on Facebook, to the sound of your phone ringing with client demands, there is a lot of it in our connected world. Sometimes it's difficult to distinguish whether that loud voice in your head telling you what you should do for your business actually belongs to you. Are you making choices from the gut or reacting to what others know best?

The one thing I'm certain of having interviewed many design leaders is that there is more than one way to play a winning game and that even though there may be similarities, nobody's path is the same. There is no sure-fire formula. When it comes to your own interior planning, following somebody else's should—whether consciously or unconsciously—because it's the "right" or "realistic" thing, if it's not in alignment with your inner truth, will always leave you feeling stressed, unsure, afraid, angry or overwhelmed.

Being visible is about listening to the voice of your inner wisdom. It's the voice that you instinctively lean on during the creative process, but that many designers turn off in the name of doing business. Often that's because its guidance is the antithesis of those right, realistic shoulds, the opportunity cost your left brain is busy calculating. It may speak quietly, nudging you to pass on a job that isn't a good client fit, despite the financial payout. It may roar with a yes for a trip to Italy now, when your accountant tells you next year. It may be uncomfortable to trust its suggestion that you live in the uncertainty of a question as you grow, especially when your left brain is demanding security.

But your intuition, that gut sense, comes from the same source where your vision began. It's not an impression. It's not what you think you know. Its guidance always comes from within and is beyond intellect. Although understanding it may seem illusive or tricky, it's always available and always right.

> How comfortable are you being visible?
> Take the quiz at mebydesign.com.

When the Faucet Turns Off

Money is currency and currency is energy. So in an esoteric sense, making money is about flow—hence the term cash flow. Understand that money is *supposed* to flow in and out of your business. However, if you are obsessively focused on the flow of money out, it will never feel like you're bringing in enough money. Focusing on what you don't have can stop your flow of income completely. If your faucet of income and/or opportunity has turned off, it's for one reason: to get your attention.

Focus on what you want and you will get it. Focus on what you don't want and you will get that, too. It is impossible to think two contradictory thoughts at the same time. So if you're living (and thinking) in fear of an imagined financial disaster, if you feel like you're broke even though you work hard or that your competitors are getting your slice of the pie, if you're constantly worrying about where your next client is coming from, you've got a case of lack consciousness.

When your faucet has turned off and you catch yourself in life's feedback loop, it's an opportunity to lean back and analyze what your lack of income and/or opportunity is trying to show you. Some designers exhaust themselves working with clients who are less than ideal, and charge less than their value to serve them. Afraid to say no to jobs that suck, they subconsciously hold off new projects so that they can take an emotional timeout from doing business. This is a subtle form of self-sabotage in the same vein as procrastination, and although it offers a temporary solution, it's not a long-term fix.

In other cases, designers aren't heeding the call for expansion. They've been in business for years but aren't confident enough to take it to the next level by going after more challenging jobs and saying no to the small ones. They get stuck on the how; rather than risk a mistake or imperfection, they dig in their heels. I also see this with designers who are afraid of technology, social media, new team structures, or investing in outside consultants. Some lower their prices, taking the slowdown personally, which is usually the exact opposite of what is required.

At the root of this flow stop is fear. Fear shows up in the form of excuses (because deep down you know that's what they are) about why your behavior can't be changed. Fear also shows up in the form of indecision, worry, and procrastination, which allows you to delay your good.

It's too late
I'm too busy.
I don't have time to try something new.

Or as imposter syndrome when your inner monologue tells you that you're a fraud.

I'm not talented.

I'm going to screw this up.

My work is not important enough.

I used to think that successful people weren't afraid. I've since learned that they get scared but take action anyway.[1] Fear can be an indicator that something is wrong, but it also might be telling you that something is right, that it's worth the risk of expansion and growth. We've already spoken about permission to want what you want. On the flip side is resistance to receiving it. Are you available to receive what it is you say you want for your life and business?

If you've been busy in the past and are bored with the projects you're getting now, chances are you need to strategically level up your brand positioning and raise your fees.

Remember, imagination without implementation is hallucination. Change is life's only constant, and trying to hold it back is impossible. Did you know that the only physiological difference between fear and excitement is the exhale? Fear causes you to take a sharp breath in. So does excitement. The difference is that when you're excited you release the breath so that your body can resume its natural flow. When you're afraid, you hold on to it for dear life. What's more terrifying, taking baby steps in the direction of the business and life that you want? Or staying stuck, unavailable and invisible? Take a deep breath and let flow.

Pricing by Committee

When it comes to your pricing, everyone has an opinion and sometimes the voices of your clients and peers will ring louder than your own. You may know what other designers are charging for their services, their mark-up, discount, and that they would never ask for X, Y, or Z. That may be helpful market research, or not, but is it proof? Kind of. It's proof that it worked for them.

But I've heard this big name does it this way. This is how it's done. Really? Have you seen a spreadsheet? Talked to their accountant? Do you know what impact their decisions have behind the scenes? Are you creating a course of action based on the actions of others whose blind spots are the same as your own? Or are you asking yourself the kinds of questions that get you to your number? Because what really matters is how much you need to charge to sustain your business and grow your life accordingly.

A good indicator that you're out of pricing alignment is that you attend seminar after seminar about pricing and keep asking other people what they charge. This state will often get in the way of your ability to close sales, keep your pipeline full, and invest in expansion. If your perceived internal value is not aligned with the external price you set, whether it's too high or too low, this insecurity will persist until you get clear on what you're worth.

Why You (Think You) Don't Have Enough Money to Market

The truth of the matter is that some people won't get the value of what you do no matter how well or often you explain it. You don't have to worry about those one-off conversations; sometimes it's not about you. However, if you can't get cash to flow or you find yourself having to prove the value of your services over and over again, it's all about you.

I know, I know, they're not getting it! But apparently, since you've had this conversation more than once, you aren't either. In fact, you're available for it (and at a subconscious level, likely getting something out of it). Take a closer look at what's going on and you'll notice the other person is mirroring a belief that you've got buried in your consciousness, one that your work isn't valuable, or at a deeper level, that you're not enough. Beliefs are simply thoughts you've practiced over and over. When your faucet has turned off, it's because the limiting ones are in direct conflict with what you say you want. The good news is that changing your beliefs is possible. It just takes practice.

For example, if you're attracting nickel-and-dime-type clients, investigate how you are being cheap with yourself. You claim to want to work with affluent clients—more on what you actually want in the next chapter—but you think you don't have the money to upgrade your online materials, invest in photography, hire a brand strategist, or network at a level that will put you in the company of said affluent clients. You price yourself low, so low that you are unable to hire the support staff you need to serve at a high level. If you do, you don't take a salary and then wonder why you feel broke, chained to your business, or why it feels like you're working for your employees instead of the other way around. (Note: you are!) Why would this affluent client you seek invest big bucks in your firm when you can't invest in yourself?

Feast or famine is a mentality. If you're not satisfied with what you make, require more of yourself, and make it a must. If you think the things you've always thought, you will get what you've always got. Why not practice a new belief that you are paid the full value of your services and that money flows in and out of your business when you need it? Set a new number.

Remember, Elsie de Wolfe grossed commissions of $100,000–$300,000 at time when the largest class of incomes was between $3,000 and $5,000 and only 800 people in the United States earned between $100,000 and $150,000. That was 100 years ago. But she didn't have to deal with the internet, you're probably telling yourself. No, she didn't. She had to deal with war—in fact, two world wars over the course of her career, as did Syrie Maugham, who also was not afraid to charge for her talent.[2]

Why You (Think You) Don't Have Enough Time to Market

Another common excuse designers offer for not taking action to level up is that they don't have the time, or that it's not the right time to begin. Time is the great equalizer. We all have the same amount of hours in a day. Time worry is an extension of lack consciousness, as in there isn't enough of it. It's also that all-encompassing excuse people use to keep themselves invisible.

Most designers are so obsessed with time that they forget they have a choice how to use it. The top complaint I hear is that there isn't enough time to be creative. The next is that their hard work isn't paying off fast enough. They're waiting for the perfect time to take a chance. While they're sure it will bring success, they're also afraid of how success will affect their time once it arrives.

Conditions will never be perfect enough for you to start what you're avoiding starting now, because perfection is impossible to achieve. Which is why you may as well get started now. If you've had the thought, "I'd really like to do this," or "Wouldn't it be nice to have that?" and you follow up that thought with "someday," what you desire is available, but you're getting in the way of receiving it. I'll bet you make plenty of time to support your clients, partner, and kids, so why is making time to achieve your business goals so complicated?

Parkinson's Law says that work expands to fill the time available for its completion. In other words, if you have only thirty minutes to write a newsletter before a client comes into your office, you will finish writing it—that is if you keep your word to yourself to be in integrity with your time. When it comes to implementing the vision and marketing for your interior design business, your calendar is your best friend. Someday never happens without action today.

Whatever you know about time, what you don't know about it is also true. So if your relationship to time isn't working, if you're tired of rushing or if life feels stuck, now is the perfect time to change it.

Overwhelmed

Chances are if you're overwhelmed, you're in the middle of a big shift from business as usual. But come on, are you really crushed and rendered helpless, which is the definition of overwhelmed? No, you're not.

Overwhelm is for people who aren't taking action to unfold their vision. Overwhelm is for people without a plan. But most important, it is for people who are refusing the support available. That goes for those of you who feel like you're treading water managing day-to-day tasks and have lost sight of the big picture.

When you're feeling overwhelmed, it means that there are ideas, conditions, rendezvous, and all kinds of cooperation ready to assist you, but you've decided you're going to do it all by yourself. In other words, you're being resistant. Focusing on your lack of time and overloaded schedule is only going to multiply those feelings.

If you want your life and business to shift, it will require you to tell a different story about the way you're spending your time. First, replace "have to" with "get to do." Remember you have the choice to be in business, a privilege many people, especially women, don't have in certain parts of the world. Next, start accepting that high-level support that is available and really wants to get to you.

> "Above all, a great designer has the power to seduce, inspire, and, when necessary, intimidate contractors, artisans, business partners, the press, and, of course, the clients who write the checks. No matter how disarmingly self-deprecating or soft-spoken he/she might be, there is no such thing as a major decorator who's a pushover."
> —Marian McEvoy, former editor,
> *Elle Décor* and *Veranda*

Mark Your Boundaries

Value and time management issues are a consequence of a condition that runs rampant among creative people: poor boundaries. Boundaries, literally the marked limit of the playing area, let other people know how you're playing the game of life and what you're available for. They keep you powerfully aligned with your vision and make sure that you take care of you.

Boundaries also set the tone for how you want buyers to treat you. Have you set your prices to do more than break even? Are clients texting you after hours? Do clients contact your vendors or trades directly in spite of what your contract states? Setting boundaries in a way that fits the way you offer services is the difference between a loyal following that gives good word-of-mouth and looky-loos who only want your services when discounts are deep.

Many designers are highly intuitive and have high emotional intelligence, which means they try to please others first, without a second thought. They feel guilty for saying no, or apologize for taking a stand on their pricing. They over-deliver. They can't imagine charging a premium for their creative services, especially when their creativity comes so easily.

For those who consider themselves artists first, this can get complicated because of a deep-rooted belief that their gifts are meant to be shared. I get it. But I also know that you can't share your gifts if you are depleted, and that too many creative people stop practicing their art altogether because they can't figure out how to support themselves while they do it. However, the old starving artist paradigm is being shattered now that creative people have unprecedented ability to reach their audience. More on that in the next chapter. Do you find yourself saying:

I don't want to, but X needs my help.

It only took me a couple of minutes to design.

I can't charge that much.

If I raise my prices, nobody will buy it.

I don't want people to think I'm a bitch.

I want to be nice?

If the answer is yes, then you're likely crossing an internal boundary, one that you haven't voiced. Let your yes be yes and your no be no. Ask yourself what the cost of staying invisible will be. Putting a value on your services and time creates an expectation that others will as well, and the amount they're willing to pay you is directly related to how much you value your time and your work.

If you need to be nice, you need to reframe what it means. According to Merriam-Webster, someone who is nice can be exacting in requirements or standards. Nice, huh? Define yourself as someone who has a nice or well-executed vision and then put powerful boundaries in place to help you stay your course. When you focus on what you want instead of what you don't want, your vision and the steps you must take to unfold it become clear and, often, downright easy.

Of course, taking a stand doesn't always make you popular with the people on the receiving end of your no, but guess what? They'll get over it. I'll say it again: in a flight emergency, there is a reason why you are instructed to put on your own oxygen mask first.

A Focus Experiment

At first, focusing on what you want instead of what you don't want feels like a paradox, simple and impossible at the same time. Start with an easy one: parking. The next time you drive into a crowded parking lot and find yourself swearing about the spot you can't find, flip the thought. Tell yourself, "Parking please. Show me an open space now, please!" When I play this game, I usually find parking within a few seconds.

Once you've mastered finding parking spots, try changing your thinking with something that has bigger stakes. For example, if you're stuck during the design process and catch yourself focusing on the stuck part, stop and flip your thought to the solution. Ask, "What would solve this problem?" Then go on to something bigger like a job size, new team member, or something from your vision list. Depending on how open you are to receiving the solution, and letting go of what you think you know, you'll come up with one immediately. It's going to take a while for you to catch yourself thinking about what you don't want, but once you do, you can use this stop and flip game in any circumstance for unexpected results.

Claim Your Calendar

One of the best ways to improve your visibility is to change your relationship with your calendar. Your calendar keeps your vision on the schedule at the forefront of your life. It holds the combination of creative time and marketing time, or beauty, meditation, nap, and workout time that you require to prosper. You wouldn't easily cancel or change a meeting with a client once it was scheduled, so don't do it with an appointment you have with yourself.

I often recommend that clients dedicate certain days to specific aspects of their business and if possible, keep left-brained and right-brained tasks together. For example, perhaps Friday morning is dedicated to bookkeeping and the afternoon to creating a prospect list or writing and scheduling a newsletter for the following week. Are Tuesdays and Thursdays new client meeting days? Do you schedule vendor appointments the first and third Thursday of every month? What day is your phone turned off? You need at least one full day without phone interruptions. The rhythm of your jobs

STYLE
Sheet™ CALENDAR ACCOUNTABILITY

Use the calendar exercise to plan out a good week, the kind of week where you feel like everything got done and you enjoyed it! Start by answering the questions below to get real on exactly where your time is going. Then use the worksheet to plot out what an ideal week looks like. Keep in mind that implementation is a process. Get one day down and then add another one.

1. On most days, is how you spend your time congruent with what you say you value?

2. Do you stick to a schedule?

3. Do you calendar everything—even gym time, grocery shopping, and date night—or do you simply flit from task to task according to what you remember or how you're feeling and hope to get it done?

4. Do you have time scheduled for marketing, including lead generation, returns, design, accounting, client meetings?

5. Are you spending your time working with ideal clients?

6. Are you taking every job, despite a full calendar or without a true understanding of what's coming up, because you're terrified money is going to stop coming in?

7. Are you always late?

8. What is the task you most enjoy in your workday? Do you do that every day?

9. What is the task you least enjoy in your workday? Can it be delegated?

10. What is your biggest time suck? Are you willing to break a bad habit like compulsively checking email or Facebook?

11. Does your family respect and value the time you've set aside for work?

12. Do you have creative time on the calendar? Creative/play time is an essential renewal for creative people.

 Download an easy calendar grid at BrandingInteriorDesign.com.

may change, but commitment to a calendar will keep your life consistent and flowing forward.

Use the calendar exercise to plan out a good week, the kind of week where you feel like everything got done and you enjoyed it!

Done Is Better Than Perfect

Designers are notorious perfectionists. They stop themselves from submitting to shelter publications or from having their work photographed because they don't think it's good enough. I don't know a creative person that isn't opinionated, even quietly, which makes sense. Our standards give us a distinct POV. But chances are your desire to get it right means you're judging yourself too harshly.

Before you cared about what anyone else thought of your work, you did it for yourself. Remember? Think about the moment you realized you were creative. Fantastic, wasn't it? How about the moment someone said, "I love that?" Were you able to receive the compliment? If you want more visibility, you must be able to receive more praise, more attention, and the opportunity to do more with your talent. If you're not sure about your work, it will be difficult to ask people to pay you for it.

Expressions of creativity and interpretations of beauty are as diverse as the people on the planet, which means designing the perfect room is impossible. My perfect ten and yours probably aren't the same. So when it comes to my creative work, instead of asking myself if it's good enough to share, I now ask myself if it's done. How you feel on any given day can impact how you feel about your work. Some days you may think you're a creative genius. Other days not so much. Chances are, though, you can definitively say when something is finished without judgment. Done comes from your gut and isn't subject to the same kind of creative insecurity.

Not everyone is going to like your work; that's a given. How somebody else judges your interpretation of beauty is their business. Your business is to use your creative gifts, fulfill your obligation to your client, and finish designing their home. And even if it's not as good as (insert the name of the designer whose work you use to beat yourself up), what does their vision have to do with you? If you've listened to what the space you're designing requires and paid attention to your instincts, and your client didn't thwart your original plan, chances are it's good. You wouldn't have been hired if your skills were sub-par, right? So why not take a scout shot or two and send it to an editor? I believe that part of the gift of being creative is to share it.

The Company You Keep

Florence Schust, nicknamed "Shu," studied under Eliel Saarinen while she was at Cranbrook Academy of Art. Like other architects of the organic movement, she wanted to relate interior design to architecture, furniture, and human scale, but she referred to herself as a "meat and potatoes" furniture designer. She said she designed the fill-in pieces that no one else was doing. By no one, she meant her friends Eero Saarinen (Eliel's son), Harry Bertoia, and Ludwig Mies van der Rohe.[3]

When Florence met Hans Knoll in 1941, he was establishing his furniture company and she moonlighted for him while working in the offices of Wallace Harrison in New York. Knoll designed unitized wall elements, chests, files, desks, counters, display cases, room dividers, and seating. Two years later Hans and Florence formed a business partnership. In 1946, they were married.[4]

With Florence's design skills and Hans' business acumen and salesmanship, they grew their company into an international arbiter of style and design. In the early 1950s, as the company grew, it became apparent that furniture suitable for public spaces and lobby areas was needed, and Florence asked her former teacher, Mies van der Rohe, for the rights to produce his Barcelona chair and ottoman, designs he had done in the 1930s. The production model was an immediate success and became ubiquitous in new buildings. By 1951, she put Harry Bertoia's line of wire chairs into production.[5]

Her friend Eero Saarinen was troubled by the "slum of legs" in modern living room settings. He insisted that a chair should not only be unified as an object but it was incomplete without a person sitting in it. He also considered the design of the chair in relation to the proportion and scale of walls, floors, ceilings, and the room's overall spatial proportions. It was an issue that caused him years of experimentation, finally culminating in the Pedestal group of 1957, also released by Knoll.[6]

The revolutionary Knoll Planning Unit team, led by Florence Knoll were responsible for the interiors of some of America's largest corporations, including IBM, GM, and CBS.[7] She defined the standard for the modern corporate interiors of post-war America and introduced modern notions of efficiency, space planning, and comprehensive design to office planning. She ardently maintained that she did not merely decorate space. She created it.

More than collecting designs, the Knolls collected designers. They began a dynasty with people they knew, designers who were obsessed with the craft, with bringing forth a new movement and philosophy. Their company provided a forum for avant-garde ideas and successfully merged profit-making with creativity. Even after the death of her husband and the company's many ownership changes over the years, Knoll's legacy of innovation lives on.

The late Jim Rohn, entrepreneur and motivational speaker, said, "You are the average of the five people you spend the most time with." Who are the five people closest to you? Because when it comes to your creative vision and business, they are definitely impacting your results. Do they uplift you? Are they innovative? Do you collaborate with ease? Are they fearful? Do they complain about how TV is killing the industry, about the internet, about everything?

If it's a team member, do you take her home every night, worrying about her after your business day is over? If it's a difficult client, is he impacting your ability to serve the rest of your clients well? Are you spending so much time thinking about problem people that you're attracting more like them instead of doing the creative work you were born to do? What is the design problem you must solve? What legacy do you want to leave?

Now I'm not suggesting that if you're married to Bitter Bob, or Debbie Downer is your best friend, you just dump them from your life. But keep your vision of expansion to yourself while you're planting the tiny seeds that need to take root. Practice changing the subject when a topic makes you feel vulnerable, or that you don't want advice about. When you are learning to listen to your internal guidance for the first time, your voice may be a quiet one.

"It makes no difference how many people you have working for you, but it makes all the difference who is working for you."
—Sister Parish

The same goes for surrounding yourself with the right support staff. Add team members with high-level skill sets that are different from your own and who reflect your values, understand your vision, and are on-brand with your aesthetic. Pay close attention to fit. I often suggest that my clients pay less attention to references and invite their final candidates into the office for a paid day or two—an office audition—to see how it feels to work with them in the role. Do they take direction well? Are they quick to pick things up? What is their energy like with other team members? Because here's the thing: if I've listed someone as a reference, it's because I know they're probably going to say good things about me. We won't get started on the folks who lie and use friends or family to put in a good word. Even if the references you get are 100 percent glowing, or conversely if they aren't, that has nothing to do with the relationship you're going to have with your new hire. Fit is deeply personal.

Make sure your team members aren't wearing too many hats, and if they are, make sure they're happy wearing them. Chronic staff turnover in any one position often means that the position is not structured properly. You may also have some internal work to do when it comes to leadership. Are you micromanaging? Are you communicating the running list you've got inside of your head? Be honest about your shortcomings and hire team members that will fill in the gaps. I've found that designers who are still establishing their POV don't release the creative reins easily to another designer and may constantly butt heads. While you're learning the components of your style, I suggest hiring a project manager and a design assistant to help you execute on the details of your vision, instead of another designer.

Interns can be a wonderful addition to your office, but only if you have the time to teach. That's the true spirit of why they come to your office, so be honest about your needs and take your mentorship role seriously. If you don't have that time, hire someone who can read your company procedures manual, figure things out, and hit the ground running.

The outside consultants you hire must have expertise in the areas you're hiring them for and be working inside the parameters you've set around your goals and vision. Is the advice you're getting up to date? Conversely, just because someone is young and knows how to use social media doesn't mean they know how to use it strategically to generate prospects. Surround yourself with people who are in it to win it, who are better than you are at the jobs you're hiring them for, and who will support you at every level of your game.

> "A decorator should, in addition, be blessed with a sixth sense—a kind of artistic alchemy which endows the articles of furniture with the elusive quality of livableness which transforms houses into homes. No amount of training or schooling, I believe, can teach you this. Either you have a flair or you haven't."
> —Rose Cumming

Your Credentials

If you've always known you were going to work in design and pursued post-secondary studies right out of high school, I applaud you. For the rest of you who found your way to the design profession after a previous career, perhaps because you didn't know it existed; thought you couldn't make money at it; or thought it wasn't important enough to pursue; you are here now. If you're self-taught, stop wasting your time worrying about the education you didn't get. Some of the biggest names in our industry— Kelly Wearstler, Martyn Lawrence Bullard, Barbara Barry—don't have formal design education. It hasn't stopped them from building lucrative design empires.

I've also worked with designers who were labeled with a learning disability and carried that shame for years. If that is you, it's time for a reframe. Some visual people learn differently. Research points to links between artistic talent and difficulties reading and writing. Leonardo da Vinci, Pablo Picasso, Agatha Christie, and Albert Einstein were dyslexic. So are Charles Schwab and Richard Branson.

One study found that self-made millionaires are four times more likely than the rest of the population to be dyslexic. Forty percent of the 300 millionaires who participated in the study had been diagnosed with dyslexia, and people with dyslexia are often very good lateral and strategic thinkers.[8] They process differently, are intuitive and excel at problem solving. They see the big picture—in other words, they are heavily influenced by the R-directed, feminine side of the brain.

You may learn by making, and that is powerful. Look at books. Go to museums, art galleries, and theater. Watch video. Travel. Do whatever inspires you to expand your mind and skills. A note to those with two or more post-secondary or graduate degrees who are thinking about one more certification: if you love school, keep going! But if you think another degree will prove you are worthy of the next level of success: it won't. Why do you think the education you have now is not enough? Go back and reread the section on understanding your value. You may find your answers there.

"O, beware, my lord, of jealousy;
It is the green-eyed monster which doth
mock The meet [sic] it feeds on."
—William Shakespeare

The Green-Eyed Monster

When Iago spoke that famous line to Othello, it was about jealousy between lovers. However, jealousy is an emotion that creative people know well. Its root implies to boil, ferment, or yeast, which is not surprising since it usually bubbles up hot and fast. It's that feeling of loss, real or imagined, that someone or something you believe to be yours has been taken away. In Buddhism, it's the inability to bear the accomplishments, success, or good qualities of others due to excessive attachment to your own gain and the respect you're not receiving. It's a consequence of comparison, and it sucks.

She got published, with that project? Who does he think he is, charging that much? Why on earth would anybody give her a fabric line? (Gossip. Gossip. Gossip.) He sold his book? To whom! It's too late for me. I'll never have that kind of success.

It's not a question of whether jealousy will happen—it's been observed in babies as young as five months and across species—it's what you choose to do when it does. First of all, understand that jealousy means you're out of alignment, because alignment always feels good. Pay attention to your energy, because your negative focus certainly doesn't impact the success of the person on other end of your bad juju.

Next, accept that jealousy is just information. That somebody else has something you want for yourself but don't think you can have. If you're in passionate judgment of someone who is doing exciting projects because of their connections, making big money, or (selfishly) spending time on their own self-care instead of on their family, making them wrong has less to do with them than it does to do with you. Stop making yourself wrong for what you desire and claim it for yourself.

Whatever nastiness has taken hold, the fastest way to dissolve it is to understand that another person's success has absolutely nothing to do with your own. Your vision is yours, and it is impossible for any other person to usurp or receive what has been intended for you, unless you allow it. Outside a religious context, faith can be defined as confident expectation. Expect to receive what you've seen in your vision.

Alignment is not a race. You still have time. The only thing limiting your opportunity is your expectation. You don't have time to look longingly at someone else's life; you need all hands on your deck. Why not risk telling the truth about what you want? Why not be open to a new strategy to get it? Stop thinking you know it all. If your peers are getting what you want, be thankful that success is in your neighborhood and that now you have a friend to show you the ropes along your way.

Take Credit

If you are a woman reluctant to call attention to your accomplishments among a group of men, you are not alone. A new series of studies says that women resist calling attention to their accomplishments when they work in groups with men, unless their roles were explicitly clear to outsiders.[9] Interestingly, credit issues disappear when women work with other women.

Perhaps you don't want to say anything because the architect who hired you has a big ego and you don't want to risk future jobs with him or her. Perhaps you don't like confrontation. Most women attempt to resolve disagreements without direct confrontation.[10] Until the last few decades, women have been socialized to play by the rules—be likable, be quiet, be seen and not heard, and get it right, which is counterintuitive to the disruption and innovation at the core of the way the right brain processes information. I believe this contributes to our imposter syndrome. We often feel conflict between who we know ourselves to be and who the world wants to see.

Asking to be recognized doesn't have to be a fight; it's simply mastering a conversation you might not be used to having. We live in a world where credit matters, but in collaborative work, it's not always clear who's done what. The next time someone takes credit for your work, take a deep breath and get in the touch with the source of your creativity. Next, instead of making an accusation, ask if they were aware that they didn't credit you. Was that intentional on their part, or an honest mistake? If they don't offer to remedy the situation, provide them with the language they can use to describe your role going forward.

If not getting credit or recognition is a pattern in your collaborations, it's time to do some deeper work. Do you give credit to others when it's due? If you're not stingy with them, why are you stingy with yourself? Why are you available to be invisible? Were you schooled to be humble? Humility comes from the Latin word *humilis* and literally means low, which is probably why you feel like you're held down. Who made you wrong for expressing your creativity and experiencing pride and joy in that expression?

Are you in the habit of dismissing the value of your ideas until somebody else sees fit to acknowledge them? You can't blame them for claiming the value of what you won't. Can you receive a compliment?

Do you see your ideas as the expression of your truth, creativity, and unique POV? Ask yourself why harboring another person's lie about your role in the process is more important than speaking your truth. If you're worried that they'll never refer you again, you have to decide whether the tradeoff of silence is worth it. Remember, no one client, vendor, or person is your source unless you let them be.

During my research for this book, I stumbled across a quote wrongly attributed to architect Julia Morgan. Morgan was the first woman admitted into the architecture program at the famed École des Beaux-Arts in Paris, and was one of the first female architects in the United States. In Beaux-Arts fashion, she designed each building from the inside out; the exterior was of secondary importance, which made me smile.

A Morgan building could come equipped with custom-designed buffets and bureaus, tables, chairs, lighting, fixtures, even dishes and linens. Morgan met Phoebe Apperson Hearst when she returned from school, unknowingly beginning an involvement with the Hearst family that would span three generations. She was the architect for William Heart's spectacular castle in Northern California, "La Cuesta Encantada," Spanish for the enchanted hill—more commonly known as the Hearst Castle—which overlooks the village of San Simeon.[11] She designed 800 buildings throughout her career, a legacy rivaling her contemporary, Frank Lloyd Wright. She also built an extraordinary variety of institutions planned for women's use. But unless you live in Northern California, you may not know her name. Because although she won a fair share of medals and mentions while she was at school, when she returned to the United States, Morgan chose to remain anonymous.

The quote that originally led me to her was false, since it turns out that she steadfastly refused to be interviewed. Morgan also did not enter competitions, write articles, submit photographs to architectural magazines, or serve on committees, dismissing these activities as those for "talking architects." She was invisible outside her circle of clients and peers.

Perhaps her admiration for the anonymity of the medieval artisan was at the root of her unwillingness to appear in print, or because at the turn of twentieth century, she was one of only a handful of women in architecture. Morgan didn't believe her ideas were revolutionary or outstanding. She had great skill in accommodating the tastes of her

middle-class clients, but because she was reluctant to push beyond what they wanted, her practical and pleasing solutions kept her far from what was considered cutting edge at the time.

In one of the only interviews she gave, to Marcia Mead, another architect, she said that women architects have "done sincere good work along with the tide" and that "undoubtedly some women greater than other architects will be developed." Blinded to the potential influence of her own vast body of work and role in history, she went on to say that women had contributed little to the profession.[12]

Morgan paid good salaries, helped the children of some of her employees with the cost of school, and shared the profits with her team when she had a good year. This collaborative model was unusual and deemed "not a practical working model for most contemporary firms." Today it's a hallmark of feminine leadership. Women-owned firms in the US are more likely to offer workers flex time, tuition reimbursement, and, in smaller companies, profit sharing.[13]

Her draftsman, Louis Schalk, who had worked in Morgan's office since high school, criticized her for selecting prospects for their personality and who were less experienced than she was. In a letter that went on for more than three pages, her former protégé upbraided her: "No doubt you have often wished for at least one girl who would amount to something. . . . There are no reasons why girls should follow up architecture in preference to marriage, but there are many good reasons why they should do just the reverse." Morgan considered her team family, and her decision to mentor female staff and hire based on personal connection seems obvious now. Studies have shown that most women join companies with the desire to be part of a team, and that they favor collaboration over competition.[14] Although she didn't change her business practices, Morgan carried that letter for more than half a century, and it was one of the few papers she preserved. As a group, women tend to register stressful events more strongly than men do. This characteristic makes it difficult for a woman to forget a cutting remark or tough feedback.[15]

When she closed her office in 1951 at age seventy-nine, she asked the building caretaker to burn her blueprints and drawings. She thought they would be of little interest to anyone except her clients, who already had copies. She spent the last four years of her life in the care of a nurse-companion who had no idea of what she'd accomplished. She retired to her small bedroom, faced the wall, and closed out the world until she died.[16]

I can't help but wonder how many more women Morgan would have found to hire and mentor if they had known she existed. She evolved in a time when it was considered improper for women to work, and yet she built a company. Her use of natural materials and building technologies seems progressive today, and her sympathetic response to her clients is a much-needed lesson for many architects. If only she could have felt how revolutionary she was being.

Women now make up twenty-five percent of the architecture profession in the United States, yet forty-two percent of architecture-school graduates are women.[17] By comparison, I wonder if there is a disproportionately large number of women in interior design because designers have more leverage to break the rules, to misbehave, and to highly achieve in an industry where no box of behavior has been firmly set for them. Use this freedom to your advantage. Speak your truth. Claim your work and accomplishments and if you can't find the courage to speak for yourself, consider speaking for that woman whom you may never know, who will see your work, learn your story, and be inspired, or for that eleven-year-old girl who looks up to you and wants to design things when she grows up.

Although we live in a time where we can own and profit from our creativity, there is a historical absence of women's voices in the arts and a legacy of invisibility and silence embedded deep in our consciousness. Enough already. The internet has given us unprecedented access to the people who need our work. Use it and let them find you. If not you, who? If not now, when?

"You have to really believe
not only in yourself; you have to
believe that the world is
actually worth your sacrifices."
—Zaha Hadid

Full disclosure: people are going to talk about your success. That's one of the byproducts of being visible. But the reality is, whether or not you're successful, they probably already do. Everyone's got an opinion, which means they're bound to have one about your fifteen minutes of fame. So what?

The late Dame Zaha Hadid, the greatest woman architect in the world and among the greatest architects of all time, was a visionary, painter, furniture designer, artist, and leader. Hadid spoke her mind and didn't filter her displeasure, often to the detriment of her public image. "I'm a woman, which is a problem to many people," she said. "I'm a foreigner, another problem. And I do work, which is not normative, which is not what they expect. Together, it becomes difficult."[18]

The media often portrayed her as an abrasive jet-set diva, but as she famously responded, would they have called her a diva if she was a man? [19] Those she cared for described her as true, loyal, and someone who "never forgot her friends." When Hadid was named to *Time*'s annual list of the world's 100 most influential people in 2010, Donna Karan wrote, "To me, Zaha's womanliness is what makes her designs so compelling. She brings a female sensibility and a goddess's touch."[20]

The first woman to win the Pritzker Prize in 2004—the architectural equivalent to the Nobel Prize—Hadid went from the architect who never built anything to the architect who in the last decade, has built everything.[21] She grew up in a Bauhaus-inspired home in Baghdad and studied mathematics at the American University of Beirut. She began her formal pursuit of architecture in 1972 at the Architectural Association in London, a student of Rem Koolhaas, who famously called her "a planet in her own inimitable orbit."

"When he said it at the time, I was upset. But in a way he was right," she said. "I should not have a conventional career and he was absolutely spot on."[22]

Hadid launched her own practice in London in the late 1970s, wanting to create buildings that would "sparkle like isolated jewels." She wanted them to connect, to form a new kind of landscape, to flow together with contemporary cities and the lives of their people. Although she gained attention for her theoretical work, her earliest concepts were considered too avant-garde to be realized.

"It has changed a lot—thirty years ago people thought women couldn't make a building. That idea has now gone," she said.[21]

The point is that as you step out onto the edge of your creativity, you will receive feedback, both positive and negative, and your ability to fulfill your creative projects will be contingent on your ability to remain visible. This is about a contract you've made with yourself to be fully expressed. Are you honoring it?

Unless it's blatantly libel—and there are ways to deal with those jokers—readers usually don't invest much confidence in the opinions of anonymous haters posting in the comment box. You don't have to explain why you're growing, just be yourself. You can't say the wrong thing to the right person or the right thing to the wrong person. As you grow into your ideal vision, you will gradually change to fit the new story you're writing for yourself.

During this time, some people find that their friendships and role models shift. It can be uncomfortable because people like us for who we are, not always for who we want to be. Go with it. The life you were meant to live is the one you choose, not the one that well-meaning people would choose for you. It's your story: write it in your own words. As you grow and continue to revise what you're available for, align yourself with people who are supportive, who value your goals and dreams with the same level of respect that they value their own, and who will cheer you on. The people who have chosen to be on board for your lifetime will come around.

And don't underestimate the confidence and pride that comes with being visible. Seeing your name in print can give you goosebumps. Winning awards is sweet. Although your ego might momentarily take up more space, ultimately you'll end up being the person you've always been, with the added benefit of being fully expressed and well-paid. That's what being a leader means.

"Every woman in America thinks she is a born interior decorator. They all say, 'I want to give you complete freedom but...' My whole life has been one long battle against those 'buts'."
~ William (Billy) Baldwin

Clients That Fit 4

The customer is always right, right? Interior design is the ultimate service business, and it's likely you learned this adage at some point as the key to your business success. The phrase became popular in 1914 with maverick retailers like Harry Selfridge and Marshall Field during a time when misrepresentation in sales was rife, when the common legal maxim caveat emptor—buyer beware—ruled the day.[1] If you've been in business for any length of time, however, you know that some clients are dishonest, have unrealistic expectations, and are most definitely very wrong for you.

Ask a designer who their ideal client is, and many will answer a rich one. But here's the thing, Paris Hilton and Warren Buffet are both rich. If you market to them in the same way, you won't reach either. Another common answer is baby boomers. But a fifty-six-year-old divorced female entrepreneur without kids, and a seventy-eight-year-old retired CEO who uses a wheelchair and his sixty-eight-year old wife who was a stay-at-home mom, would all be considered boomers. Each has entirely different priorities and requires a different conversation to close a sale.

When you get it right, branding your design firm shortcuts the buying decision for clients who are a fit for the way you do business. Communicating the value of your services will require you to dig beyond the surface of these broad target market generalizations and tell the story of your business in a way that embodies universal human truths like the desire to feel successful, safe, or at home. It's also going to mean getting personal. While this may come naturally to savvy designers who have mastered the in-person sales conversation, this level of mastery doesn't usually extend online. Because when it comes to the web, social media, and email marketing, most designers have no idea who they're talking to.

> "What is most personal
> is most universal."
> —Carl R. Rogers

Everyone is willing to pay more for something, as long as it speaks to a longing in their soul, and those kinds of longings are too big to be crammed into just one adjective: affluent. Design is a transformative process, not just inside the home but inside the soul's of the people who live in them. In other words, messy. Choose clients who you can confidently help to navigate that process, whose version of crazy you understand.

Although demographics matter, determining what is personally relevant to your ideal client matters even more. Why have they decided to build that dream home? Are they travelers with more than one residence? Has an illness or health issue made universal design a priority? Are children part of the story or have they just flown the nest? Are they avid collectors of fine art, antiques, or furniture designed by artisans? Do they want their children to inherit the collection? Does sustainability matter? Do they want a showcase garage for their car collection or are they tech moguls who demand a fully wired home? Why now? Why is this gut renovation, new home purchase, or fluff-up happening today?

Just as the answers to these questions will impact your vision for a space, the answers are also essential in crafting authentic and precise communications for design brands. Perhaps you specialize in hospitality or have a high level of patience and compassion when it comes to working with the elderly. You may be a LEED AP or specialize in turnkey vacation properties. Figure out what your ideal client longs for and let them know why the services you provide will make their lives better. Include that in your sales conversation and copy and you'll have a slam dunk every time.

Remember, even though the service you provide is all about them, it is rooted in a platform that is all about you. When it comes to finding clients that fit, what you value as a human being, and the reason you're in business in the first place, are the things that will resonate with them. (If you're still not clear on your *why*, revisit chapter 2.) My guess is that the clients you've most enjoyed working with have a high level of trust in your vision and ability to execute it. How did they describe their experience working with you? What were their deal breakers? What were they afraid of and how did you soothe their fears? Although "affluent" or "baby boomer" may have been included among the list of words you used to describe them, they probably wouldn't be the first words that came to mind if I asked you to describe the quality of your personal relationship. Those are the qualities you need to put at the forefront of your marketing.

Tiny Tribe, Big Influence.

You don't have to speak to an audience of thousands to get business. Instead build a tiny tribe that you can influence. Tribe is a term that Seth Godin made popular in his 2008 book of the same name. According to Godin, the internet has ended mass marketing and revived this social construct from the past. A tribe is a group of like-minded people connected to a leader by way of shared values and ideas. For design professionals, this connection is also about your vision. The success of your leadership is predicated on your ability to engage your tribe, in other words, to be in relationship with them based on your design philosophy and all that it entails emotionally and aesthetically.

As an example, an Orange County interior designer I worked with started posting products she thought her ideal client would love to her Facebook business page. She posted a rug with a short comment saying she'd like to use it in a bedroom. Shortly thereafter, a past client reached out and hired her to use the rug in a guest bedroom redesign. When I asked how many "likes" her Facebook business page had, the answer was just thirty.

When it comes to your tribe, use the Pareto principle, more commonly known as the eighty-twenty rule: twenty percent of your ideal clients will give you eighty percent of your sales. Think of it this way. If your average minimum budget is $100,000 and you earn thirty-five percent of that, just three clients will net you a six-figure year. Why not work with clients who are the right fit?

The easiest way to nurture your tribe is to start with one person. Who is the client that best fits your working style? Getting hyper-specific about your messaging and tailoring your tweets, Facebook posts, blogs, and newsletters to this person creates a magnetic pull. Because when you truly understand what your ideal client wants, you will reach others who have similar soul longings.

Keeping your ideal client in mind also means that you won't feel like you're randomly posting information online. Because you're not. Every time you tweet, pin, or blog, you will be in conversation with that one person, or in some cases a couple, and you can ask them to help you in ways that will increase your success.

Thinking about designing a new product? Ask them about their color preferences. Want to build your list? Ask them to sign up for a monthly newsletter where you will offer tips, photos, and inspiration. Then ask them to share your offer with their friends. Want them to follow you on Twitter? Offer them something in exchange. Once you know who your ideal client is, you can target your marketing dollars to reach them in the places you are most likely to find them both online and offline. Give and take, ask and receive. When you're sharing with a real person that you care about, they want to hear from you.

But if I'm just speaking to one person, isn't that going to narrow my client base?

Nope. For example, I write my weekly newsletter to just one of my clients. I write to address her problems and give specific advice about growing her business and about leadership, something that is important to her. I will often receive emails from others on the email list who ask if I wrote that newsletter for them. Even though my clients represent a wide range of aesthetics, at their core, each shares my ideal client's desire to be a leader. Since creative leadership—in particular, creative women's leadership—is my passion, most prospects culled from my list are compatible with my working style. Because I know my ideal client looks forward to my newsletter and because I have a high conversion rate from it, I put a lot of effort into that part of my marketing. It's a win-win for everyone.

I've never worked with an ideal client. Now what?

If you've just launched your business and have no idea who your ideal client is, market to yourself as if you had the budget to spend on your own services. Do you like what's in your portfolio? Are you attracting the nickel-and-dime types because you're cheap with yourself or because deep down you believe people can't afford your services? If you can't figure out why you haven't worked with an ideal client yet, revisit chapter 3 and tackle your visibility issues to the ground.

Revealing your preferences authentically and transparently is the fastest way to build your brand and attract clients who resonate with your work. Use Pinterest, Instagram, Facebook, and your blog to hone your visual style and showcase it at the same time. You can add layers to your ideal client profile by thinking of someone you really get along with now—like your husband or best friend—and assign the qualities of your relationship with them to your ideal client profile. The key here is to be specific. Always have somebody in mind when sending out communication about your business. You can always change who you're speaking to later.

How Exclusive Are You?

Ideas about what makes a luxury lifestyle have evolved in recent years. But just because you're branded as a luxury firm doesn't mean that clients with an open checkbook will show up. Although the notions of limited or rare can still command premium pricing, communicating the value of luxury interior design services lies in understanding the fundamental differences between marketing luxury goods versus luxury experiences. Which are you selling?

"Luxury experiences are by far the most powerful driver of luxury spending everywhere. Collectively, they make up nearly $1 trillion of the annual global total," says Jean-Marc Bellaïche, a former senior partner at Boston Consulting Group and co-author of the firm's third flagship report on luxury branding. "As older consumers realize that they have all the 'things' they want — and as younger people favor experiences they can share with their friends — consumers are spending more on everything from dining at five-star restaurants to exotic vacation travel."[2]

New luxury is never about price, overindulgence, or pedigree. Instead, it's about personalization, customization, and intimate, unforgettable experiences. In many cases, prospects who seek experiential luxury tend to be less interested in visible displays of status like expensive watches, cars, and jewelry. For luxury car owners—and luxury vehicle advertisers always hit the mark—a purchase confirms that they have made the right decision and reaffirms their status as members of an elite and privileged group.

Prospects who seek experiential luxury are usually fulfilling the need to be something. A stay at a luxury spa or resort, fine dining, and vacations in exotic locales make for good stories to tell, but the rewards—instant pleasure, self-confidence and security—are not always visible to others. With this in mind, designers who brand themselves as luxury must package their services as something personal that unlocks the customer's values and highlights who their client can be. What are benchmarks along the continuum of that experience? How will the client feel on the other end of their home's transformation? Tell them a story about themselves in their home that they won't be able to resist.

Educate Before You Decorate

Education is another important piece of a designer's sales conversation as the market for interior design grows online. A Google search will return "modern lamps" but it can't distinguish between 1950s, '70s, or what modern means now. That's where you come in. Perhaps your potential client knows only what they've read on their iPad, or seen on a TV design show. That doesn't mean that they're not ready to make a sizable investment in their home.

In 2013, Scripps Networks Interactive and Vision Critical released the findings of a random survey of 1,000 people on home-related topics such as real estate, renovation, decoration, and budgeting. More than eighty-one percent of the people surveyed believe that "money spent on improving my home will show a good return," while sixty-six percent agreed that "now is a good time to invest in my home." In fact, Americans love their homes so much that sixty-one percent indicate that they would "choose to spend on their homes rather than on something else like a vacation or the latest electronics." And here's the kicker: only one out of five is confident that they are knowledgeable enough to keep a contractor honest. That means four out of five people need your help. But if you're talking down to these prospects because they don't understand the process, or what it really costs to design a home, you're unlikely to win their business. Have you intimidated them about the process or made them wrong about watching television programs that may have sparked their interest in seeking you out? Teach them that there is a difference between entertainment and the real design process and that your expertise in navigating it smoothly will pay back their investment tenfold.

Understanding who your ideal client is will help you decide whether additional qualifications can help your brand be a leader. A Certified Aging-In-Place Specialist (CAPS) has learned the technical, business management, and customer service skills essential to home modifications for seniors. LEED AP (Leadership in Energy and Environmental Design) or Green Associate certification from the US Green Building Council will establish your credibility in the green building marketplace. The CHID appellation from the American Academy of Health Care Interior Designers (AAHID) is considered the benchmark for health care interior design work.

"You can tell almost at once
whether you can work together;
if you can cope with it, if it's worth it,
if you can make the house one they
can live in comfortably—and when
you've both decided if you can,
it may be only a matter of days
before you both realize there's
been a terrible mistake."
—Sister Parish

One of the keys to attracting and maintaining high-quality relationships with clients that fit is to set clear expectations with your communication. If you don't have a welcome kit, create one that outlines your firm's etiquette. What are your hours of operation? Do you have a no-texting policy? What about your policy on custom orders? Some of this may overlap from your contract, but it's a good idea to highlight the important parts of your process separately in easy-to-read language so that your rules are always top of mind.

Outline your design, procurement, and implementation schedule and set expectations for client decision deadlines, especially if there is a drop-dead delivery date. I also suggest sending clients a round-up email at least once a week that documents the progress on their project during that week, what your next steps are, and what's left to complete. Even if you're still waiting for orders to arrive, let them know. For those of you who like hands-off clients, they will be more likely to relax if they know you're on it. It also creates a paper trail you can use if anything goes wrong.

Assign a team member who will be responsible for communication and for scheduling appointments between you and your clients. The busier you get, the more important it is to create a separation between you and them unless it's with respect to high-level tasks. Make your assistant or project managers your point people. As often as possible, reserve one or two days each week for handling client calls and meetings. Reserve the rest of the time for driving the creative process forward.

The Good News About Bad Clients

The good news about clients that aren't a fit is that they create an opportunity to improve your business systems, procedures, policies, and contracts. Worked with a client that hovered during the install? Rework your contract to make sure that when the time comes, they go out of town. Did you forget to take project creep into account when you negotiated that flat fee? Next time, make sure your contract states that your hourly rate will go into effect after your negotiated timeline expires. Did they refuse to pay you for travel time? What does your contract state with respect to travel? Did they ask for a refund on a custom order? Have them initial your "no-refund on custom order policy" in your contract and then reiterate it in your welcome package. Did they try to hire one of your vendors directly? Ask your lawyer to draft a contract clause to make sure it doesn't happen again.

Now, I'm not saying you shouldn't ever work with someone who doesn't meet your ideal client profile, because that profile will be in constant evolution. The kind of clients that helped you grow your sales to six figures will probably not be the same clients who help you grow them to seven. Exceptions always exist, but the key is not to feel like you have to do business with someone who isn't your fit to succeed. Revise your online and offline communication at least quarterly to reflect your growth and preempt the business behavior you don't want by specifically outlining behavior that you do, and never ignore the red flags.

Do clients complain about all of the previous designers they've worked with? Do they ignore the time boundaries you've set? Have they refused to give you their budget? No matter what they tell you, every client has a number. If they refuse to tell you theirs, they are not ideal. Release them. If they are genuinely unsure, let them know yours. Does your average room cost $50,000 or $100,000? Is that a fit? Before you even agree to meet, make sure that you've set the expectation for what it costs to do business with you so there are no unwelcome surprises down the road. If you can't answer the question yourself, don't be mad at them for not understanding your value.

I know you've got bills to pay, but never take a job because you feel like you have to. It's never about the money. That's right. Ask yourself, if you had a cushion in the bank, would you still want to work with this person? Are you setting yourself up to deal with a royal pain (RP) who saps the joy out of your creative process and makes it difficult for you to serve others at the highest level that you are able?

No one client is your source. Get on board that wealth consciousness boat I talked about in chapter 3 and reprogram your mindset to believe that there are more than enough clients available for you. The same is true if you're feeling guilty for saying no. Consider this: If you think the process will be difficult for you, it will likely also be difficult for them. Release them so they can find someone who works in a style that complements their own. Make a conscious choice about whom you will serve, how you will serve them, and who can be served by somebody else.

Few of the housewives who hired Dorothy Draper to bring color into their lives wanted quite as much color, and quite the same colors, as Dorothy Draper, or "DD," wanted to give them. Rather than becoming trapped by her clients' tame taste, she started chasing spaces other decorators weren't interested in: hotels and resorts. This project sector became her true life's work, the work that would make her famous. As for those housewives, Draper wrote them a book.[3]

You may not seek fame but I do know that you want to be fully self-expressed, so don't be afraid to say no. Often saying no gives you the space you need to receive the idea for your next level of expansion and the time to step into it. It internalizes your commitment to changing your course. What is it that you've stopped doing in expressing your creativity to please the wrong clients? Give that up, now.

The Affluence Trap

The nature of the design business is emotional, but take your emotions out of the negotiations.

But they don't have a lot of money.

That's what I heard from a consulting client who had who met with a doctor couple with a pair of kids in private school and a house on the water near San Diego. They had bid on her services at a silent auction and needed help with their dining room. She'd fallen in love with them and the possibility of transforming their home. She was also excited about the photos she could get and the slew of referrals the wife promised to give her once the project was complete—that is, if she cut them a break on her design fees.

I don't want to charge them too much because I want them to hire me for the rest of the house.

One of the biggest mistakes design professionals make is discounting the price of their services now because they're excited about the prospect of referrals later. First of all, the referrals you'll get will be based on the fact that you're cheap. Next, there is no guarantee that you will complete the job, complete the job to the client's liking, or that you will want their referral at the end of the process. The only question you need to ask: is this a fit now?

I totally get it. Wealth, abundance, and your perception of it is deeply personal and often irrational, but service and servitude are two entirely different states of being. How does it serve you when you buy into somebody else's money story? Why is your financial security less valuable than the security of your client's? What about your kid's tuition or the renovation you want for your home? You make those experiences difficult to receive when you don't charge for the full value of your services.

Take yourself out of your client's money story and examine the facts. According to Census Bureau data, only twenty percent of American households ever break the six-figure mark. Those who do join the ranks of a segment dubbed the mass affluent, new rich, or HENRYs (high earners, not rich yet).[4] This group—doctors, lawyers, consultants—is the professional and entrepreneurial class that drives the economy. They're relentless strivers who work incredibly hard to build their careers and move ahead. They don't need to worry about making a mortgage payment or a credit card payment, but they probably don't indulge in the toys owned by the ultra rich. That's because they don't think of themselves as rich. If they live in Washington, Boston, Los Angeles, New York, San Francisco, or Seattle, where the cost of living is higher than most other American cities, they're probably not rich—at least they feel like they're not.

This group that many call affluent shoulders a bigger tax burden than other segments of the population. After they pay that tax, they probably don't have a lot left for housing, private schools, saving for retirement, and paying down the student loans that earned their professional status in the first place. But you don't have to feel sorry for them, because this group that represents the top twenty percent of US households took home a record fifty-one percent of the nation's income. They also account for nearly forty percent of total US consumer spending and about the same percent of design industry spending.[5]

In a 2013 survey of 100,000 Houzz users, the leading online platform for home remodeling and design, only eight percent of respondents hired a designer based on the cost of their services. Eighty-eight percent hired them because of great reviews, because they were experts in their field (seventy percent) and then because of fit or personality (sixty-seven percent). Professionals respect other professionals. Expect as much from them as they do from themselves. They figured out how to pay to go to a good school, live in a good neighborhood, and drive a good car. They value home and they want a beautiful one. Trust in their ability to figure out how to pay for your good service.

Lean Back

When it comes to negotiating, lean back. If you really want a job and more than one designer is competing for it, you may be tempted to lower your fees to win it. In other words, you've leaned forward in the negotiation, creating a pick-me quality of desperation that leaves you imbalanced. If you catch yourself in this state and can't command the language to turn things around, lean back physically. Try it now. Sit up straight. Square your shoulders, open your chest and lean back. Do you feel more powerful? Studies show that body language not only communicates what you're feeling but it can also change your body chemistry and impact your ability to perform. Leaning back literally requires you to see things from a new vantage point. It gives you a small window of time, perhaps enough time to remind yourself why you established your fee structure in a certain way in the first place.

Practice Gratitude

The best way to find and work with the right clients is to practice an attitude of gratitude. Be thankful for the client experiences you've had that went well and focus on them. And if you've had a traumatic client experience, let that memory go. Too many designers focus on that one nightmare client and throw themselves into an emotional loop that they are doomed to repeat because those stories loom large in their consciousness. Perhaps you had a bad experience with a wealthy past client who treated you poorly, and now you hold a grudge against every other wealthy person. Again, focus your attention on fit. The past is over unless you keep choosing to activate it in your present.

Use the worksheet to identify your ideal clients and define the qualities of your relationship with them. Get really honest. The more specific you are, the more it's going to feel like this kind of ideal client relationship couldn't possibly exist—that's a good sign you're on the right track—but it does. Hint: you've already worked with them.

Revisit the ideal client worksheet at least bi-annually or if your income changes dramatically to make sure you're still talking to the right person wherever they hang out on and offline. People are constantly changing, dynamic beings. The more specific you get and the more precise your marketing and communication, the more likely they are to find you.

Clean Up the Mess

1. Make a list of three clients who were difficult to work with and in one sentence sum up what went wrong.

2. What personality traits do these clients have that do not complement your working style?

3. List at least one way you can improve/revise your policies, procedures, and/or contract so you don't experience the same problem again.

Finding the One

1. Make a list of three clients you've loved working with.

a. List every trait they have in common, whether it's age, income, gender, marital status, job, lifestyle, or project budget.

b. Dig deeper. How did they find out about your services? Why are they starting the design process now? Do they have more than one residence? Is this a first or second marriage? If they donate to charities, which ones? What kinds of books do they read? How do they get news? Getting inside the mind of your ideal client will help you figure out how to talk to them.

2. What personality traits do these clients have that complement your working style?

3. How did they describe the experience of working with you?

4. Combine the information from your answers to create your ideal client profile. This one person or couple has the sum total of all the characteristics your three favorite clients have in common.

5. Get to know everything about your ideal client by making a vision board or Pinterest board that tells your client's story. No detail is too small. What do they drive? What neighborhood do they live in? What labels do they like? Do they collect art?

6. If your business has a split focus and serves both residential and hospitality clients, do the worksheet twice, listing ideal clients in each specialty. For example, if you primarily service new construction, your ideal residential client may not be the same as your ideal builder client. In that case you will still market to one decision maker but you will market to them separately.

Generate New Leads

1. List three places your ideal clients spend time online (Yelp, Facebook, LinkedIn). Don't know? Ask them.

2. List three places your ideal client hangs out offline (such as philanthropic organizations, church, sporting events).

3. If you were going to speak to an audience of your ideal clients, what would you talk about?

To listen to the audio version of this interview with Vicente Wolf, visit www.soundcloud.com/mebydesign.

Vicente Wolf on Ideal Clients

An award-winning interior designer, product visionary, art collector, author, and world traveler, Vicente Wolf has built a global luxury brand serving the right clients. He has been recognized as a design leader by every major shelter publication in America, including *Architectural Digest*'s "AD 100," *Elle Decor*'s "A-list," *House Beautiful*'s "10 Most Influential Designers in the United States," *Traditional Home*'s "Top 20 Designers of the Past 20 years," *New York Spaces*' "Top 30 Designers," and *Interior Design*'s Designer Hall of Fame.

For Wolf, a successful space is always in motion—an open system that can be visited by the occasional shooting star. His list of projects is an interior designer's bucket list of hotels, retail spaces, apartment buildings, and private residences across the United States and in France, Israel, Japan, Saudi Arabia, and Sweden. He does it all from a light-filled loft in New York City with a team guided by integrity, simplicity, and his passion for design.

When was the moment you decided to become an interior designer?

VICENTE WOLF:

Well, it's really what led me to that. I had gotten fired at every job I'd ever tried and was running out of situations. I mean, I had certain shortcomings. I am dyslexic. I never finished high school, and I am Cuban, so I was a refugee in this country. Although I had a creative inkling, I didn't have the papers to walk into a career, but I was lucky enough to meet somebody who was involved in the industry. It touched on what my childhood had been—my parents were in the construction business in Cuba. I had been looking at plans, scaling rooms, and watching buildings go up since I

was small, so it was familiar. I started sweeping floors in a showroom and ended up forty years later quite happy to be in the industry.

Your journey is pretty incredible. So let's talk about the creativity. Strong, sensual, light-filled, comfortable, cool, luminous: these are some of the words used to describe your rooms. Is there a predominant emotional experience you want people to receive from your projects and products?

VICENTE WOLF:

It's not something that comes consciously. I'm a firm believer in working from the gut, and so creating environments is very instinctual. I like

Below: Interior design and photography by Vicente Wolf

spaces that bring a sense of calm. As the saying goes . . . water seeks its own level. The clients want that for their own homes, so that's how we sort of meet. It's worked pretty well through the years. I seem to create environments that have those common denominators.

Do you have a favorite or memorable project?

I think that there are favorite clients, such as Clive Davis and Michael Lynne. People who taught me things and gave me the pleasure of being around them while they were being who they are. How else would we have ever met these people if it wasn't for what we do, and how lucky we are to be touched by these people and walk away with amazing experiences. That is more important than what the bedroom looked like.

You've built a global brand. How much of your company's vision was from the gut versus being strategic, and is it easier or scarier to take risks now?

VICENTE WOLF:

It's not about taking the risk, it's about keeping up with your standards—am I still as creative as I was five years ago, ten years ago—and always trying to meet that goal of pushing myself to really be as good as I have been.

I always was not very social but hardworking, so I was more comfortable working than going out. It was as a sort of complete focus on what I was doing, because I love what I do, and it's not what most people would call work. It's really pleasure. I love designing. So it just sort of fed on itself.

The biggest thing is the travel, because I love to travel and I think that has kept the creativity alive because each time you're experiencing

Below: Interior design and photography by Vicente Wolf

different situations, it gets your mind thinking about things, how to approach something in a different way, how to look at things differently. That was really the thing that has kept me moving forward because there's always a new place to go and new things to see.

What would you say to designers who find it hard to say no to projects that are financially unrealistic because they want to be published? In those early days when you're trying to get the work and you're trying to survive as a company, how important is it to say no?

When I started it was a very different time than it is now. There was a very small group of designers that were doing modern things. Everybody else was very traditional and so the magazines came to us because it was news. Now it's just so incredibly competitive.

When you give somebody something for nothing, they never respect you. I think that you need to maintain some sort of standard of what you can do and what you can't do. I think when they're trying to get you to do a whole apartment for $2K, you're not going to be able to achieve it.

So I think it's very hard and I think that many times they take advantage of people who are just starting. "Well, I'm going to give you a break," or, "All my friends are going to see you." What I always say in those situations is, let's just deal with your project. What may come later will come later, but this is about you and about your project and let's focus on that.

The most important thing is that designers have to have a contract, have to act professionally, have to be very clear business people besides creative people. If you don't, you may be the most talented but if you can't run a business, if you don't know how to sell your ideas, you're not going to succeed. You're always going to be struggling and I think that you need to really have all your ducks in a row to really succeed. It's sad to say, but I think that the creativity is really the low man on the totem pole, because it's the professionalism, it's how you sell it, and the high level of taste. The higher level of taste you have, the harder it is, because your vision is not usually the common denominator.

So it's getting all those other things polished and done right that makes the clients respect you. When you have a contract; when you're laying all your requirements down on paper; they know that this is not a hobby, this is a business, and I think that when you don't do those things, I think that you're doing a disservice to the industry in general.

Vicente Wolf Home is the luxury showroom where Vicente displays his line of fabrics, lighting, upholstery, case goods, and accessories that he hand picks while traveling the globe. Call for an appointment at the showroom, (212) 244-5008, Monday through Friday and visit them at 333 West 39th Street on the 10th floor in New York. Find him on Twitter @VicenteWolf, on Instagram @VicenteWolfDesigns, and on Facebook. com/Vicente.Wolf.

"Don't be intimidated by audacity.
Be audacious—but with taste."
~ Madeleine Castaing

Build Your Online Home

Once you've defined your personal brand and know what you're talking about and to whom, it's time to build your online home. Your website is one of the most important tools you have to market your services, so make it a reflection of the highest vision you have for yourself and your business. Experts expect the number of people using the internet worldwide will exceed the current global population by 2020, with access to broadband and mobile phones set to rocket.[1] A visually memorable online presence creates a halo effect when it comes to doing business with strangers. That means a visitor who likes one aspect of your brand will have a positive predisposition toward everything about it. In other words, a website with wow factor wins.

A Brand by Any Other Name

What's the best name for your design firm? Should it be an eponymous firm like Vicente Wolf, Kelly Hoppen, or Clodagh? Or should you claim a separate brand identity like Dwell Studio or Commune? Ultimately, the decision is as personal as the way you do business. Your name, your initials, or a derivative of your name if the spelling is tricky, is the easiest choice. Some designers are hesitant to use their own name, thinking it may not be memorable or interesting enough to brand a firm. My feeling is that if you can walk through life with it, you can definitely hang it on a shingle. Use "interiors" or "interior design" to qualify your type of firm—for example, Kim Armstrong Interiors rather than Kim Armstrong Design, which could be a graphic design, fashion design, or product design company. If you run a multi-disciplinary studio and plan to do products, events, art, or installations, the latter may suit you.

If you know that you want to sell your company later or are concerned about privacy, using another name to build a stand-alone brand might be a better choice. If a firm in another state has the same name, don't use it, especially if that firm owns .com, the extension most people search first. You risk frustrating and confusing prospective clients who want to get to you, and you could also have trouble if you try to trademark the name later. Besides, if that many people thought of it, it's not a singular brand. Your URL is no-cost advertising. If you decide to create a separate brand identity for your business, it is still important to purchase the URL for your legal name. It's another way potential customers can search for you, and you can point that secondary URL at your home page. Your email address is also free advertising, so set up yourname@yourURL.com and stop marketing for Gmail, AOL, or whatever internet provider you use.

Finally, if you're not absolutely in love with your name choice, don't use it. Even though you can rebrand later, you will have to take the necessary legal and financial steps in addition to communicating the change to your clients and vendors. "Formerly known as" is a waste of copy for firms that were barely visible in the first place.

Making Your Mark

Your mark or logo must be consistent with the energy and identity of the brand you are building, and it's one of the first things potential clients will see when they arrive on your home page. Famed logo designer Paul Rand said, "A logo is less important than the product it signifies; what it means is more important than what it looks like."[2] Whether it's an icon, hand drawn, or a text logo, every time it shows up anywhere else in your marketing, whether it's on a Facebook page, mobile phone, or stationery, it must be consistent in appearance, size, scope, color, and feel. The best logos aren't complicated. They tell a story and are meaningful at first glance.

A tagline, also referred to as a slogan, motto, strapline, or endline, can be placed underneath or adjacent to the logo. A tagline is a short and snappy phrase meant to compress the meaning of your brand's vision, competitive position, product benefit, and promise into a convincing story. A tagline says something about who you are and what makes you special. It resonates strongly with your intended audience, letting them know why they should care about your company. It's not written in stone and can reflect a change in positioning or a relationship with a new audience. However, the best of them act like the final exclamation point wrapping up your thirty-second company pitch.

A growing school of thought says that taglines have diminished in importance. In fact, half of Forbes's "Best-Loved Advertising Taglines" ran before 1975 and many brands—Starbucks, Whole Foods, Nordstrom—don't have them.[3] Can you remember the tag for your favorite interior designer? Shorter attention spans have prompted a shortening of ad copy, and in today's media landscape, where 140 characters or six seconds of video delivered via the tiny real estate of a mobile phone screen rule, taglines can crowd out the brand logo.

Too often designers try to tack on a tagline to an undefined design brand, as if that phrase will give them market value and meaning. But a tagline won't help a brand that's been poorly defined. If you're branding from the inside out, and you haven't done the work to define your vision, it's going to be difficult to come up with something that defines it succinctly. If you have more than one tagline in your marketing material, or if you're trying to distinguish yourself according to products and features rather than value and personality, skip the tag and focus on defining the way you offer your vision.

Laying the Foundation

At minimum, your website home page should link to pages for your firm bio, personal bio, information on how you work with clients, portfolio images, and contact information. If you work from home, you may want to use a PO box for privacy and safety. You will also want to include your Terms & Conditions in the footer. We'll talk more about those in chapter 8. You'll also need an up-to-date photo of yourself alongside your biography. Potential clients want to look into the eyes of the person who will be rifling through the dark, hidden corners of their homes. Think of each of the menu items listed on your home page as rooms in your home. Keep them clean. Don't clutter them with unnecessary copy.

Whatever additional pages you choose to add, whether it's press, a blog, testimonials, products, giving back, a list of speaking engagements, or brand collaborations, every page should add layers of information and build trust with your audience. One of my biggest pet peeves is clicking a menu item and being delivered to a page that says "under construction," which is often the case with products, shops, or a blog. The coming-soon approach is not an effective form of advertising. I know you have plans, but that tab announces that you don't know how to finish them. If you have a hard deadline for your launch, consider including a landing page to collect email addresses. Once you have full content, you can let visitors know you've added these other elements.

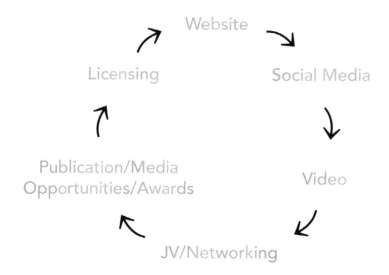

A Portfolio Story

Your logo may be fantastic, but if your portfolio photography sucks, attracting a high level of clientele will be difficult. The same goes for all that home page text your computer geek wants you to add. You're in a business where image is everything, and telling your story visually with high-quality images must be your priority.

During West Week 2012, Margaret Russell, former editor in chief of *Architectural Digest*, told an audience of industry professionals that good photography "is not a luxury. It's a calling card. It's a business tool." In other words, if you've ever taken your own portfolio photos to save money, stop. Editors aren't looking for good enough; they're looking for wow. Wow sells magazines. But wow photography is not only key to winning editorial opportunities, it's an important tool for building your archive. If you decide to write a book later, you won't have to start from scratch.

A designer in Pasadena learned that the hard way, when a prospective client shared that, "(He) thought he could afford me because I didn't do high-end photography. The bigger fish are used to working with designers. The lower-end client has sticker shock over and over again."[4]

Your portfolio will likely be the first impression a potential client has of you. If you can't bother to showcase your own work at its best, what message does that send to clients about how you'll treat their home? Now, I get that everyone has to start somewhere. But if you've just launched and you're bootstrapping your business, don't junk up your portfolio with images that are low-quality or off-brand. Set the tone with one or two shots using the highest quality camera you own and leave your prospective clients wanting more.

Label your portfolio according to geography and project type to help with SEO—for example, Hamptons Beach House or Houston Condo. Save your cell phone photography for your iPad presentation and before-and-after shots. Before-and-afters usually beg for a story, especially if the photography is not professional. Share those process-oriented photos on your blog or in a newsletter where you can speak to your methods and product choices.

Never underestimate the power of energy and resonance when it comes to marketing, and use caution in showcasing photos of rooms you don't like or that don't express your aesthetic. Are you really interested in doing more rooms like that? Because that room you don't love influencing your next potential client's decision to hire you.

Stock photography is also a no-no, as is—I hope it goes without saying—the work of other designers. It's an infringement of their copyright, and illegal. If you'd like to use work you did at another firm, get permission and credit the other firm. Depending on the agreement, include the photographer's name under every photo. The same guidelines apply for rooms by other designers that inspire you and that you feature on your blog.

Photo Ready

Hire a photographer who specializes in interior design, keeping in mind that there are differences between architectural, interior, lifestyle, real estate, and portrait photography. The right photographer will have a sensitivity to capturing the heart of a room. Not all architectural photographers shoot people well, and vice versa. A good lifestyle photographer can often toggle the line between both worlds. Lifestyle and portrait photography is shot tighter; more is left out of the frame, which means more is left to the imagination. The most powerful images are usually the ones that provide just enough information to trigger a daydream. For example, the way the sun hits the side of a couch, a beautiful blanket, and the newspaper makes you feel like it's a casual Sunday morning.

Make sure you and your photographer have a similar communication style and that he or she understands what you want. Pin or cut out images to show what you'd like to achieve. You've spent months getting the details of this home right; take the same kind of care when you tell the story visually. Create a shot list and, if time permits, do a walk-through. Understand the publication you're pitching to and make a list of non-negotiable shots. Then get out of the way. If you've hired a pro, you won't need to micromanage the shoot. Allow for the photographer's interpretation and collaboration.

Whatever mood you're trying to strike, don't scrimp on the support to make your pictures beautiful. That means hair, make-up—definitely—and also wardrobe. Always be photo ready. I can't stress this enough. Not only will you be more relaxed for camera, but it ups the ante on your professional game, especially if you hate having your picture taken. Keep additional accessories on hand so you can swap things in and out until you get the right composition for the frame. If you're targeting a specific publication, think about hiring a photographer and stylist who have worked with the publication before. Styling for camera is different than styling for a room. Sometimes you've got to pull a chair closer to the camera, or switch out the pillows, or even eliminate a favorite accessory because it's not working in the photograph. It can take an entire day to get ten great shots, and hiring a stylist hastens the decision-making process.

Just as there is more than one way to bill an interior design project, photographers have different ways of billing for their services. Some will give you the rights to the photographs outright, along with a CD of the images. Others will give you a select few to use for basic advertising and promotion—website and social media—and charge a separate fee for use in a magazine or book. Make sure you acquire the rights to use the photos in the way you want. In our digital world, I strongly believe it is worth the investment to purchase additional rights so that you can market your business in any way necessary.

Copy Tips

When it comes to website copy, choose your words as carefully as your images. You are speaking to your ideal client on every page of your site, and that will dictate your copy's voice, length, and style. Your firm bio is the one-sentence pitch that tells prospective clients—and the search engines—who you are and what you do. For example:

> With offices in New York and Los Angeles, [your firm's name] award-winning team manages the design/build of residential and commercial projects throughout North America, in cities including: New York, Los Angeles Toronto, Atlanta, Palm Beach, Miami, San Francisco, and Aspen.

When you write your personal bio, get personal. Whether the tone is conversational or formal and written in the third person, let your ideal client know that you will be able to solve their problems. Is there an interesting personal story that expresses the kind of design you do? For example, are you a second-generation decorator or were your parents artisans or trade manufacturers? Reflect your sense of humor and the catch phrases you always use. Your opening sentence must be concise, snappy, and genius to generate online discussion. Readers will be unforgiving of poor spelling, grammar, and punctuation, so have someone proof before you post. Use your STYLESheet from chapter 2 as a guideline.

Often designers will use time in their bio as proof of success. For example, "I've been in business thirty years." This is tricky, especially if your website is dated and you don't have press, awards, or a sizable online following. You may have been in business for a while, but that doesn't mean you've been doing it with distinction. Instead, my preference is to include career milestones like show houses, press, and peer recognition in the form of awards.

If you've transitioned from another industry—and many designers have—keep the career recap brief. I've read bios of designers with backgrounds in finance, marketing, and other fields, and got a better sense of what they accomplished in the past versus now. That's not to say you shouldn't mention past achievements. For example, a past client who spent two decades as a NICU nurse and home health care entrepreneur, is using that experience to target health care clients. Here's how she related it to her ideal client—a busy hospital administrator.

> *Prior to pursuing her education and professional practice as an interior designer, she was a registered nurse, hospital department head, and owner of a highly successful pediatric home health care business. She expanded the business to five states before selling it to a national chain.*

Notice that the writing style is formal, masculine, and brief. Keep in mind that your brand's value lies in your ability to distinguish yourself from other firms and, in some cases, convey exclusivity with your premium offering. A list of the same services that other designers in your area offer—floor plans, furniture, and color selection—won't do that. I recommend that designers replace the services tab with a "Work with Me" or "How I Work" page that outlines defining elements of your process as they relate to your ideal client. For example, if you are known for your custom furnishings and you use them on every project, highlight that. If you are a LEED AP and the story of how you got there is interesting, tell it. What is it about your methods, process, and philosophy that distinguish your brand?

(Very) Basic SEO

SEO is tech speak for search engine optimization and refers to a website's ability to draw traffic. If someone types "interior designer, Ohio" into the internet search bar and your SEO is optimized, you will show up on the first couple of pages of results—those that people are most likely to click through. Google's algorithm favors sites that are mobile-friendly, which means they're easily viewed on a cell phone. The key to success on mobile comes down to load time. Forty percent of people will abandon a web page if it takes more than two seconds to load. Forty-seven percent expect a web page to load in two seconds or less.[5]

Make sure your URL is indexed on Google—and on Bing, Yahoo, and AOL if you're super keen. Indexing is the process where the bot software that Google sends out crawls through your site to collect information to add to Google's searchable index. If you're using Wordpress, the content management system (CMS) that supports the majority of personal brand sites, there are several plugins for SEO optimization. Including key words in your blog posts and the key word box on your website will increase your likelihood of coming up in the search. A two-sentence firm bio with relevant search words, including your geographic location and industry, will usually get the job done. Unless your primary landing page is a blog, don't include banner ads or other types of advertising. The same goes for pages with links to referrals. Your site is your online home and should reflect only you.

If you are set up as a blog, ask blogger friends to include you in their blogroll. When a blogger or online outlet mentions you in a post, have them link back to your website. Check those links periodically to make sure they're not broken. Finally, sign up for Google Analytics at google.com/analytics and have your developer add the tracking code to your website so you can see who is visiting your site, how much time they spend on it, and where they're coming from.

Don't make the mistake of thinking that by rigging your SEO, you will attract clients by the boatload. Sure, the right geek might be able to get you on the first page of a Google search, but what happens when that user clicks through? Do they sign up to your mailing list? Did they contact you about services? Is that how your ideal client is looking for you? Depending on their net worth and age, referrals or a community speaking engagement may be richer sources of new business. Understand who you're marketing to and their go-to source for information. If it's online search, you'll want to invest more in SEO.

Blogging 101

If you're asking, "Do I need a blog," my response is, "What do you expect to achieve with it?" Do you want a creative outlet for your ideas? Do you plan to use your blog as a sales tool to attract your ideal client? Or both?

A blog is a communication tool, and the best ones connect with their audiences because they are frequent, relevant, and engaging. If you're writing from a place of passion, a blog can be an amazing outlet, not only for creative expression but also as a way to illustrate your process with photos showing a project before, during, and after your work. If you want to write a book, a blog allows you to collect stories and practice different narrative styles, getting feedback in real time. You're also building your platform, which is important from a publishing perspective. You must have an audience who will buy your book. Organize your search categories as potential chapter headings and let the number of hits guide the book content.

Your blog is an extension of your voice and can be even more intimate than face-to-face communication. If you're just starting your business or don't have quality photography, a blog gives your reader insight into who you are as a designer. Blog about how you approach different rooms and about products you love. Include inspiration boards for projects you want to do. Share photos of your own home or vignettes you create in friends' homes. Blogs allow you to refine your POV and connect with the people who resonate with you.

The design blogosphere is an industry of its own. Some bloggers have built massive online followings that they've parlayed into interior design careers, press attention, brand collaborations, endorsement deals, sponsored posts, and affiliate sales commissions. They have also created built-in buyers for their products. Bloggers with large followings also command coveted red carpet and shelter publication opportunities.

If you're not a writer but you still want to blog, try a visual blogging tool like Tumblr. Founded in 2007 and owned by Yahoo!, Tumblr is a microblogging and social networking platform that allows users to post multimedia and other content to a short-form blog. Half the user base is between the ages of thirteen and thirty-four, and the other half are identified as "young at heart." Tumblr users connect with others around their passion points, but rather than commenting, you reblog and share it. Many of the digital boards are built around brands

Architecture is one of Tumblr's biggest search categories, and the platform is also popular in entertainment and fandom culture. If you want to be on camera and target a young audience, get on Tumblr. On average, for every four followers who reblog your content, six of their followers will reblog it also. Link the blog tab on your website to your Tumblr URL and you've got a visual storytelling tool.

A well-written blog can convert a prospect into a sale, but just as often, it doesn't. Some well-known bloggers say that eighty percent of the work of blog writing is promotion.

If your intention for having a blog is simply to drive traffic to your website, you've chosen a labor-intensive way to do it. Blogs as a means of expression definitely add value as a marketing tool, but if the last time you posted was over six months ago, you probably are not impacting your SEO. You are, however, letting readers know that you're inconsistent, and that's damaging your credibility.

Make no mistake. Running a successful blog is a full-time job. Commit to a minimum number of posts per month. Make sure the schedule is posted so your readers know what to expect. If you've decided to blog, do it because you've got something to say, or teach. Blogging about your life can be interesting and inspirational, but readers will keep coming back for the takeaway. These days, though, many are heading to Instagram and Pinterest for the inspiration they once found in blogs. If you're not consistently posting stories that express the truth of your brand and information that will be relevant to your ideal client, you are wasting your time.

Getting Social

When it comes to doing business, word of mouth has always been the Holy Grail. Social media amplifies word of mouth at scale for free. Whether you use Facebook, Twitter, Pinterest, LinkedIn, or Instagram, social platforms allow you to communicate with your audience by creating multiple narratives to engage them. If you plan to sell products, social media is the fastest way to create an audience of buyers. Social media is also proving essential to driving online traffic. Collectively, the top social networks drove 31.24 percent of overall traffic to websites in December 2014, up from 22.71 percent in 2013.[6] And social media users who receive great service are telling an average of forty-two people, compared to just nine people offline.[7]

Place social widgets—the graphic link that identifies the social platform it's attached to—above the fold and brand your social media pages in ways that are visually consistent with your website. Like blogging, social media works best when it's used consistently. Similar to a TV station, each social media channel has its own voice and etiquette. Although some platforms allow you to cross publish—for example, you can publish an Instagram post to Twitter and Facebook—you may risk turning off potential listeners if you don't customize your message to the platform.

Many designers complain that social media compromises their privacy, that it's a waste of time, and that managing it is overwhelming. The issue of privacy is directly related to your comfort with being visible. Social media requires a level of transparency, authenticity, and revelation that hasn't previously been asked for in doing business. Bear in mind that you can choose your narratives. Start slow. You don't have to share every detail of your life, just the ones that relate to your POV and process. Keep your pages up-to-date with project progress, press recognition, and new products and technologies you love. If you're comfortable making your family, lifestyle, and other personal details part of your brand voice, go for it.

In terms of user-friendliness, if you can operate the camera on your cellphone, you can do social media. The only extra step you have to master is downloading an app and hitting send: easy. Plus, the visual nature of so many of the platforms is perfect for marketing interior design and is a lot of fun for designers. With the right plan of attack, social media is actually a time saver because you can network with your ideal clients, their peers, and your vendors without ever leaving your desk.

Facebook

Facebook is the largest online social media platform in the world. On February 28, 2015, it had 1.39 billion active users. Put another way, roughly one in seven people on Earth use Facebook. Half of those users access it only on mobile. In other words, Facebook is too big to ignore.[8]

Set up a business page and make sure you've engaged the "call to action" button next to the "like" box so that visitors can choose to subscribe to your mailing list. Once you've captured their email, you can market your services directly to your ideal client's inbox when they're not online. Aim to post at least once per day and keep your posts conversational and written to your one ideal client. Don't use hashtags. Buzzsumo's study of over one billion Facebook posts showed that posts that include a hashtag receive less engagement than those without.[9]

If you have more Facebook friends than business followers, consider posting your work on your personal page, too. Ultimately, you want people who know you to share your work. Don't be worried about commanding big numbers. We'll talk more about audience building in chapter 7.

Pinterest

Pinterest is an online pin board whose value proposition is discovery and ideas for the future. The platform allows users to save images from around the internet with a click, using the easy to download and install Pinterest button for their browser. The half-life of a pin can last forever, or at least until it's deleted. The good news is that there is no correlation between the number of pinners who follow you and the impressions made by the things you pin. In fact, according to Eric Hadley, head of partner marketing at Pinterest, you're likely to get more traction with a few dedicated followers, because those people are more closely aligned with your aesthetic than your followers on other social media platforms. If a pin gets re-pinned eleven times, it will probably mean something to eleven different people. One of those could be your ideal client.

I like to think of Pinterest as a visual way to plant the seeds in your ideal client's future. Create boards that are specific to the kind of projects you intend to do for them and label them clearly so that they can find you. For example, if you want to do a Brooklyn brownstone, use that label. Make sure your profile includes your website URL, what you do, and the areas you serve. Pin your work from your website to your boards on Pinterest so that users who click the image will be directed to your website's portfolio page. Make sure your photos are watermarked with your URL and check with your photographer to ensure you have usage rights.

Twitter

I've never watched Bravo's Real *Housewives of Beverly Hills*, but I have heard about Yolanda's Fridge. Yolanda Foster, wife of composer David Foster, is billed as a "domestic goddess," and her refrigerator has become a supporting character in the popular reality series, with a Twitter account boasting 16,000 followers. If a fridge can find its audience, so can you.

Twitter is real time distributed widely. Companies with 1,000-plus Twitter followers get six times more website traffic.[10] It operates like a journalist's news wire feed and syndicates information to audiences as it happens. If you've got a blog post, newsletter, or video to share, tweeting it will increase the likelihood of it being seen. Treat Twitter like an online cocktail party. If you're looking for media exposure, follow the editors of the shelter publications and get to know them. Use hashtags to make it easy for users to find tweets related to specific content and geography. Use the "list" feature to create curated groups of editors, people you admire, vendors, or influencers. You can create your own lists or subscribe to lists created by others. Viewing a list timeline will show you a stream of tweets from the users on that list.

There's a lot of debate about whether to follow everyone who follows you back and the ideal number of tweets per day. Again, choose what aligns with your personal vision and audience size. You may build your following more quickly if you follow everybody back, but it won't guarantee the quality of your relationships; more on that in chapter 7. And there is no conclusive number regarding tweeting frequency. Some experts recommend as few as five tweets while others insist you will need to schedule ten to fifteen tweets per day to increase your reach organically. Platforms like Hootsuite and Buffer (see the resource list at the end of the book) can help you select the optimum times. But just because you're scheduling tweets doesn't mean you can walk away. The point of social media is to be social. You must make yourself available to track retweets, favorites, and comments in response to your original posts, and to interact with other people's posts.

Instagram

Founded in October 2010, Instagram has qualities of Pinterest and Twitter in that it is photo-sharing in real time, but it's a mobile-driven app. Though it can be viewed on an iPad or desktop, the functionality comes from inside your phone. More than 300 million people worldwide use Instagram, sharing 70 million photos and videos every day. This app has a lot of growth potential because it was quickly acquired by Facebook and, according to a Forrester study, delivers fifty-eight times more engagement per follower than Facebook. With a per-follower engagement rate of 4.21 percent, it has 120 times more engagement than Twitter.

Many bloggers have refocused their efforts on Instagram, and the app is also quickly surpassing Pinterest as designers' favorite platform. It's a photographer's dream because the built-in filters allow you play with lighting and contrast. Brands post an average of one to two times per day; high-performing content has a longer shelf life than average posts, so it's important to focus on quality. Devote time to creating visually interesting content rather than continuously putting out fresh content for the sake of having something new available. Because Instagram users scroll through a single stream of images, even when they're searching specific topics, your post will stand out as it ages.

Using hashtags to categorize your posts is the quickest way to grow your following; emojis can also be used with a hashtag to search. Research shows that posts with eleven or more hashtags get the most engagement; the maximum is thirty. Open the search window and type in the subject you're thinking about adding a hashtag to, and the service will tell you how many posts exist under that and related subjects. For example, #midcentury has 407,467 posts as I write this. #Midcenturyart has 3,684 posts, and #midcenturymod has 2,966 posts. If you have less than 1,000

followers, you're likely to grow your feed more organically by choosing hashtags with less than 100,000 posts.

Like SEO search terms, the narrower your search category, the more likely you are to be discovered by people who understand and like what you do. Use hashtags such as #interiordesigner #yourcity. According to SproutSocial, hashtags with location get seventy-eight percent more engagement. Give your projects in progress unique hashtags that followers can search, such as #HamptonsCottage. Add a thumbnail from that project to your portfolio section with the same hashtag. That way editors and potential clients will know what to search for.

Don't forget to post them to Facebook. A Buzzsumo study of over one billion Facebook posts from three million brand pages found that images posted to Facebook via Instagram receive more engagement than natively published images. This is particularly interesting, as often, cross-posting from one platform to another results in less engagement.[11]

LinkedIn

LinkedIn is the world's largest professional network with more than 347 million members in 200 countries worldwide, including executives from every Fortune 500 company. Although it is heavily used by college graduates, it is also the only platform whose users are concentrated in the thirty to sixty-four age bracket.[12] Upload your professional bio and a couple of your portfolios, especially commercial and hospitality if you serve those clients, because this is where business decision makers park online. LinkedIn gives you the chance to connect with potential clients, and also with joint-venture partners and vendors.

Don't underestimate the value of "lurking"—not talking but listening—in the LinkedIn groups of people with whom you would like to do business. For example, if you're looking to do business with realtors in your state, search for them geographically. The same goes for dentists, lawyers, and any kind of professional you consider your ideal client. What are they already talking about? How can your services help to solve their problems? Contribute to the conversation with honest answers to showcase what you know, and demonstrate leadership. As with Facebook, you can publish updates, but you can also write blogs posts and share them with your network. But remember, LinkedIn is business focused. Save your post about the return of macramé—a post I recently saw there—for your blog and decorating sites where it's likely to reach the right audience.

If you're still resisting social media, focus on one or two platforms. Twitter tends to be writer focused, so if you're going to write a book, use it. To tell your visual story, you're probably better off devoting your efforts to Instagram, Pinterest, and Facebook. Think of social media sites as your broadcast channels. Like network television, each of these "stations" has a different voice. If you can't see yourself getting active on social in real time, sit down with an assistant once a week and give him ideas for content that he can post on your behalf. You can also record your ideas into a tape recorder and have someone transcribe it. Then schedule posts and sign-ups to your newsletter. Make sure, though, that someone is checking in with your audience, whether it's responding to their comments or saying thank you for RTs and FTs.

Like designing and building a home from the ground up, the key to staking your claim online is to create a presence that reflects the way you do business. Are there best practices? You bet. Do a lot of folks do a lot of the same things? Yup. But just as many don't, and they still succeed. For every person who tells you that you must have a blog, or to forget about Twitter, there is another person who swears that those two tools were the key to their success. If you want to separate yourself from the pack, inhabit your online space in the way that only you can. If you want to work with amazing clients, there is someone very important you'll need to get in touch with first: you.

To listen to the audio version of this interview, visit www.sound.com/mebydesign.

Get a free website checklist online at www.mebydesign.com.

Christiane Lemieux on Brand Authenticity

Named one of *Fortune* magazine's most powerful women entrepreneurs in 2012, Christiane Lemieux revolutionized the textiles market when she launched DwellStudio in 2000. A fresh voice in the interiors world, the entrepreneur, designer, and author started one of the first companies offering home goods online. Her modern, luxurious furniture, tabletop, and kids' products quickly found an audience, including celebrity fans like Gwyneth Paltrow, Liv Tyler, Gwen Stefani, and Nicole Kidman. In August 2013, Wayfair, which sells more than thirteen million home items from 7,000 brands, acquired DwellStudio and welcomed Lemieux to the leadership team, where she continues to oversee the company. In January 2014, she was appointed executive creative director. She provides creative vision and counsel across the e-commerce leader's growing portfolio of home brands including Wayfair.com, AllModern, Joss & Main, and DwellStudio. Lemieux is also co-host of *Ellen's Design Challenge* for HGTV. Her next book, *The Finer Things: Timeless Furniture, Textiles, and Details*, will be released by Clarkson Potter in 2016.

Left: Christiane Lemieux. Photo by Andrew Southam

You started your career as a fabric assistant for Isaac Mizrahi. Is that right?

Yes, when I graduated from Parsons I took two very specific jobs. One was with Isaac Mizrahi at the very high end, kind of the luxury end of the marketplace doing fabric design and development for a fashion company.

Above: Dwell Studio. 77 Wooster Street. Soho NYC.

He was owned by Chanel at the time, so I got to work with the most beautiful fabrics in the world. The second job was at The Gap, when Mickey Drexler was the CEO. I wanted to see how a large company functioned in some kind of capacity in the design world. Two sort of binary experiences, but they taught me a lot.

@MEBYDESIGNTV:
So you always had a vision that you would have your own company?

@CHRISTIANELEMIEUX

I did, yes, but as I tell a lot of entrepreneurs, I really wanted to get as much relevant experience as possible before starting my own company to mitigate mistakes to the extent I could.

@MEBYDESIGNTV:

How did you know it was the time to go out on your own?

@CHRISTIANELEMIEUX:

The third job I took was for a company called Portico, which was happenstance. A friend whose husband was in private equity bought this home furnishings company and didn't know what to do from a product development standpoint. He asked me to come onboard principally to do surface design for their textiles, which was one of the big categories they sold. I did that, and then got fully involved in everything from packaging to furniture to overseas sourcing, to everything. I really got all the tools I needed to start my own business, and it ended up being in home furnishings instead of fashion, because I fell in love with the industry. Then I tried a couple of my designs on the floor and they resonated with consumers and I figured that was the time to make the leap.

@MEBYDESIGNTV:

Very cool. So did you start with a big investment? Did you have partners? Did you do it on your own?

@CHRISTIANELEMIEUX:

I did it all on my own. I left that business with about $15,000 in the bank. But Portico was really a visionary brand at the time and larger companies looked to Portico for trend and product inspiration. I used that as a calling card and went to some of the larger companies like Crate and Barrel, Room and Board, and sort of pitched my private label services because at that point, not only could I design things, but I could also have them manufactured. I had developed this whole network of suppliers in Europe and Asia and so I was very lucky that all these companies took a chance. That became the venture capital arm of the business, if that makes sense?

@MEBYDESIGNTV:

Just genius. When you launched your line of furnishings in 2000, DwellStudio was a pioneer in the online interior design space. Why did you start online, and do you think staking your claim there is what helped your brand gain fame so quickly among consumers? Because obviously you were doing the private label stuff from the commercial standpoint.

@CHRISTIANELEMIEUX:

We got online very early on. Just because I think that online is the future of commerce in every single respect. We're just starting to touch on the iceberg of that. I think people are going to really transition how they do business and what retail brick and mortar means, but I've always been fascinated with 2.0 economy of sales, and we wanted to be involved in that very early on.

@MEBYDESIGNTV:

How has it changed since you started out? With so many flash sale sites, have they impacted the way you do business online?

@CHRISTIANELEMIEUX:

I mean absolutely. I think that the world of online sales changes daily. It's just one of those things where you have to be willing to be super nimble. When I first started the business it was some online, but then we still had to go the traditional trade show route. So every year we would do the trade show schedule, show our product, get orders from our large wholesale customers, and then also fulfill direct consumer online. And the great thing is that people who are starting out in business today don't necessarily have to do those types of things. For young entrepreneurs there's just so much opportunity that I didn't necessarily have and that was even five, six years ago. The whole world of getting your brand out in front of people, channels of distribution, getting in front of eyeballs, has really opened up. It's a great time to be in product development and entrepreneurship.

@MEBYDESIGNTV:

From the original vision of your company to now, has it transformed a lot? Did you always expect that you would have a company this size? Your job-choosing was very strategic, what about the growth of your business?

The job-choosing was really strategic and then after that it was just the wild, wild west. I don't have a business background, so I just followed my gut and each move has been carefully considered, but I certainly don't have an overarching business plan. The sky is the limit. For me, it's about the experience, it's about the journey. It's about doing the next interesting thing. That's sort of how I've developed this thing and it's grown pretty organically.

@MEBYDESIGNTV:

I want to talk about brand DNA. For me, the DwellStudio brand is synonymous with luxe and modern. Is there a certain emotional experience you want customers to have with your brand or do you determine that on a product-by-product basis?

@CHRISTIANELEMIEUX:

No, I think there's an overarching emotional experience we want people to have with our brand and I think it's really about the personal. That's why I wrote *Undecorate*. I think the most beautiful interiors, the most beautiful design, the best kind of lifestyles, are ones that are really personal to people. So we don't prescribe that you have to buy page twenty-five of the catalog in order to have this Dwell lifestyle. To me it's more about what do you love and keeping the things you love, and hopefully mixing in some of the pieces we have, and really it's self-expression through design. There are no rules.

@MEBYDESIGNTV:

What about the designer who wants to break through?

@CHRISTIANELEMIEUX:

Do some great work and get it in front of people, because if they don't see it, they're not going to know you're there. Take the risk. Put your best foot forward. Put together the greatest portfolio you can think of and send it out. Large companies are looking for new talent all the time. I think talent is the ultimate currency. So if you feel like you've got it, then show it.

Left: Dwell Studio Interiors. Photo by Jonny Valient

Do you think press helps, getting media attention, has that helped at all?

I do, but you know what, in this day and age there's so many ways that you can get that yourself; social media, referrals, people talking about you. The most important thing is just putting yourself out there.

@MEBYDESIGNTV:

So speaking of social media, how do you use it and do you think it's important for business, the evolution of your brand, and creating a unique customer experience?

@CHRISTIANELEMIEUX:

Well, I do. I don't know that social media is the be all and end all in terms of sales and I certainly would never use it that way. I find companies that try and browbeat you via social media to buy their product—I'm not sure it's necessarily the best strategy. I really like social media to communicate with our consumer so that they know we're here and listening. I like it to communicate our authentic brand story, so there really is a real person behind this brand. It's not something that some large billion-dollar corporation made up and then tried to back into a story. There's still a lot of that now. Everyone is about story-telling, but this is an authentic brand and so it's nice for them to know that there's a person behind it who's living the lifestyle that they are communicating to you. To me, it's all about authenticity, brand story, and communicating a lifestyle. And you know what, if you want to buy the products, great. If you just want to participate in the lifestyle, great. If you just want to look at pretty pictures, great too.

@MEBYDESIGNTV:

So what do you think is the best thing and the hardest thing about being visible?

Well, I was reticent for a long time about being the face of the brand but then I realized everyone is doing it. Everyone is their own brand and so I realized it's a requisite for business in any way, shape, or form, whether it's a tiny business or a massive business. I think people are looking for authenticity and they're looking for a real person, a real voice behind the brand so they don't just feel like they're being serviced on some sort of large corporate agenda. So I've kind of done it gingerly, but to me the most important thing is again to be authentic. Be who you are, tell your story. I think there are also limits to what you want to share online. I think there's a level of what's appropriate and I think that level is different for everybody. You're certainly never going to see a selfie of me in my bikini but you know, other people choose to do that. You're probably not going to see a selfie of me at all, but you'll see the experience and you won't necessarily see endless photographs of my children, either, because that is my personal life. I'll do things that are business enhancing but beyond that, you have to draw a line. Everyone's line is different, though, that being said. You might be in the bathing suit business and a selfie of you in a bikini is massively additive to your sales. It's really your own personal litmus test.

@MEBYDESIGNTV:

Awesome. So how would you complete the following sentence, design is . . .

@CHRISTIANELEMIEUX:

Design is self-expression.

Find Christiane Lemieux on Twitter @CLemieux and on Instagram @ christianelemieux. Visit Dwell Studio's flagship store at 77 Wooster St. in New York, online at www.dwellstudio.com, and on Instagram and Facebook @DwellStudio.

"A fellow by the name of Chauncey Howell who used to be on Channel 4 news everyday, he came into a room that I did, a show house room, and he saw chintz and he said, 'Chintz, mints, lints, wince, chintz, prints, Prince of Chintz'". He said it on the news show back in 1984. It's catchy. I got a lot of great publicity out of it. They say, 'Here's the Prince of Chintz.' People say, 'Where's Chintz? Where is that country? We don't know that country.' Why have I been popular? Sleeping with editors. Sleeping with clients! (Laughs) No I think the basis of mine in particular is that I've stuck to the same thing. I've been known for the same thing. I haven't done anything else and I do it myself."

~ Mario Buatta

The Power of Press

It may be subliminal, but when a would-be client sees the tiny thumbnail of a publication they love on your website press page, it boosts your firm's brand credibility and what they're willing to pay for your services. People who say that press isn't important are flat-out wrong. Press attention is not about vanity, it's a key component of your Visibility Strategy. It also acts as a promotion and sales-generating tool, especially if you want to create passive income opportunities like licensing.

Editorial is third-party endorsement of your work. When an editor decides to publish a home you've designed, they recognize you as a leader among your peers. It's also because your story and aesthetic will appeal to their core audience of readers. Paid advertising in those publications doesn't come cheap. For example in 2016, a full-page, full-color, one-time ad in *Elle Decor* cost $104,195[1]. Multiply that number by the three to five pages in an interior design feature story, and you'll have hard numbers for what your press coverage is worth.

When I hear designers complain that they got covered in such-and-such publication and they didn't get any business from it, I usually ask two questions. First, are you absolutely sure that your coverage didn't net you any business? Just because a client didn't mention it, doesn't mean that they didn't see it, that a friend didn't see it, or that it didn't help the prospect lean toward a yes as they were weighing the pros and cons

Left: Photo by Peter Vitale

of hiring you. Second, did you do anything with the coverage? You guessed it. The answer to both questions is always no.

Local, National, International

The easiest way to get press is to start local. Local press singles you out from the professionals in your area and attracts sales close to home. Your city or town probably has a newspaper, magazine, online publication, or blog that everybody knows about. If you think your ideal client might look at it, even casually from time to time, it's worth pitching a story about your company. If there is an opportunity to write a monthly column or contribute a series based on an on-brand theme—for example, holiday decorating, or downsizing for empty-nesters—even better. Now readers will have a chance to get to know and trust you.

National publications are the next step, and because the net is cast wider, there is also more competition. It's a myth, though, that only designers in large cities like Los Angeles and New York get coverage. Look at the pages of *Veranda*, *Elle Decor*, and *Architectural Digest*, and you'll find design leaders from Atlanta, Philadelphia, and Nashville, among others. Sure, large cosmopolitan cities have a concentration of high-net-worth individuals and more opportunities to meet editors, but there are also a heck of a lot more people vying for their attention. If you're a big fish in a small pond, you're more likely to stand out. I have clients in Toronto, Houston, and Wyoming who have been published nationally.

International publications are an excellent way to build your audience globally, especially if you plan to sell products or if you're interested in working overseas with a jet-set clientele. It's also a great way to reuse publication-worthy projects that have been published nationally. Usually there are no publication-rights issues across continents. In fact, being published in a national magazine makes you more visible to international editorial scouts. And if you decide to publish a book later, international clippings show proof of platform.

How to Pitch

Pitching isn't rocket science. Whether you're pitching to a shelter magazine, online site, or TV show, the most important thing to understand is who you're talking to. Every publication has a target demographic they want to reach and an online editorial calender that lets you know how they're structuring their content for the year. Editors are the gatekeepers of stories, and an editor's criteria is as unique as her point of view. Is your work current or visionary? Are you using products that the advertisers already feature? Did you work with a celebrity who lives in the geographic area the publication serves? But the most important thing every shelter editor wants to know is whether your project been published before, and by whom?

Although it is changing, there is still a pecking order for shelter, online, and television. Because of their limited page count and printing costs, shelter publications are considered the most prestigious design press, and exclusivity is important. That means your work can't have appeared anywhere else. So make your first choice wisely. Don't pitch multiple publications simultaneously, and be sure that the publication you're pitching is a fit not only for you, but for your ideal client.

But if I can't showcase my gorgeous project on my website, how will I get work? This catch-22 is common for designers who are building their portfolio or shifting styles and want to post new work on their website. I know you're probably convinced that this one project is going to change everything, and it might, but that's a lot of expectation on one little project. There is nothing to stop you from showing that project during an in-person meeting on your iPad, and if you use social media, you can document the design process there. Waiting is worth it in the long run, especially if you're committed to having a long career.

The big benefit of digital publications is that stories live online in perpetuity after they go live, available to come up in a user search and deliver potential prospects to your website time and time again. Digital publications are also more willing to feature projects that have already been published, especially A-list ones. And, of course, digital stories are more easily viewed on mobile, so make sure that stories link back to your home URL.

Before you pitch, buy three to five issues of the magazine and read them cover to cover. Do the articles focus on the designer, the person living in the house, or both? How are the rooms styled? Do the projects skew luxury or budget conscious? If you don't have a whole home, is there a section where your bathroom or kitchen renovation can run on its own? Do you have a product or tip they can use in the front or back of the book? Check out the online portfolios of designers who have been featured to get a sense of whether your work is in their wheelhouse, but just for reference. If you're going to fixate on whether your work is good enough, skip this.

Most magazines have submission guidelines on their websites. If they don't, check the masthead—the opening pages of the magazine where the editorial contacts are listed—to determine who handles what. If you've been reading the magazine regularly, you will know that already! If you still can't figure it out, try the coordinator or managing editor.

Submit a short project description that outlines who lives in the home, the problems you are solving, and interesting project details, along with the products you used. You will also need scouting or professional photos that showcase the rooms you designed and the home exterior. You only get one chance to make a first impression. Particularly if you've never been published, work with a photographer who shoots in the publication's style and submit high-quality photography. Make it easy for an editor to say yes.

The Squeaky Wheel

Getting published is a Sisyphean pursuit, one that takes time. In fact, getting published in print can take twelve months or more from the time you pitch your project to the time the publication hits the stands. Radio silence after a pitch is common. Editors are busy, so follow up with them every two weeks or so until you get a firm no. If you're under consideration, an editor will often let you know relatively quickly, but waiting for the final decision will require a lot of patience. While you're waiting, don't market with images that are under consideration. Use your blog or social media channels to tell other aspects of the story—with mood boards, construction progress, detail shots, etc.—and keep the big reveals for the majors.

Don't forget that social media is another way to be seen by an editor. Are you following the editors of the publications you want to be featured in? Is your website and/or contact information clearly listed on your handle profiles and on your website? As a producer, one of my biggest pet peeves was stumbling across an amazing product or person, only to discover that there wasn't an easy way to get in touch. If you don't want to include a phone number, provide an email address that you or your staff check regularly, and respond to media requests promptly.

Editors Are People, Too

Ultimately, getting published represents a personal relationship you're building with an editor, one that allows you and the work you do to be top-of-mind during your career over time. So treat them kindly and get to know them like you would any other peer. Remember, even though it feels like they have all the power, they need you to do their job well and are excited about discovering rising talent. Follow them on social media. Engage with their posts and get a sense of who they are as human beings and what they care about.

If the editor of the publication you've set your sights on is speaking at an industry event, plan to attend. During the Q&A portion of the presentation, ask a smart question—stating your name and company first—and if there is a cocktail party afterward, try to make a casual introduction. Don't rush the stage, hand them your business card, or pitch them unless they've asked to receive pitches. A written note or email afterward to thank them for the time they've spent sharing what they know and what you learned from the presentation will make a more lasting impression.

With the volume of pitches that come across an editor's desk, most will have to see your name a few times before they recognize you. Chances are you won't get published the first time you submit your work, and it's important that you don't hold a grudge. No doesn't mean never. It just means not now. Don't give up. There are usually a lot of reasons your work doesn't fit that have less to do with your talent than with logistics. Keep in mind that shelters work four to six months in advance, often more. If your story is seasonal, you may have missed the deadline.

Pitching television requires less lead time, especially if it's morning news, but there is also a greater likelihood of last-minute changes. As a story producer, it was common to pull, replace, and reprogram content to accommodate breaking news, advertiser requirements, or guests who canceled, sometimes just hours before airing a segment that had been planned for months. If that happens, roll with it and know that the kinder you are, the guiltier the producer will feel and will want to make it up to you.

Advertorial Is Not Editorial

The right editorial is an essential component of any Visibility Strategy because industry professionals have chosen to stand up for you and your business publicly to a wide audience. Editorial costs you nothing. Advertorial, on the other hand, comes with a price. It's a form of native advertising that is different from traditional paid advertising, because it is presented in the guise of editorial. It often includes interviews with designers about their work but must also legally include the words "sponsored" or "paid advertising." If you've paid for coverage, don't include it under the press tab on your web page. If an editor clicks there to see where you've been covered, it's an immediate turnoff to discover that your press is paid and begs the question: what other little lies is this designer telling with respect to her work?

A full-page or half-page ad or advertorial can be effective in local or niche publications that your audience reads, depending on your stage of business. Similarly, online aggregate sites like Houzz have advertising plans that push designers to the top of the search results in their area. Similar to the use of a blog, social media, or your newsletter, there is no guarantee that paid advertising will inspire a potential client to action. If you decide to purchase advertising, make sure it's only a portion of your marketing budget. Then if it works, by all means do it again. Don't fix what ain't broke.

When To Hire a Publicist

Early in my career, I produced no-budget independent theater, which means I wore a lot of hats. One of them was publicist. I built relationships with editors by submitting well-written press releases and photography and suggested story angles, earning over 200 press pick-ups. So when it comes to designers getting press, I have a DIY philosophy. Editors are constantly looking for the next new story to tell, and you don't need a publicist to reach them.

However, there is no disputing the value of a good publicist. If you're putting off the work of being seen, consider hiring a publicist. A good publicist will never guarantee to get you published. If you don't have the projects or the POV, he has nothing to pitch. Hiring a publicist also won't let you off the hook in terms of connecting with editors, but hiring the right publicist at the right stage of your career can be very effective. A publicist is a consulting team member. If you have publication-worthy projects that are ready to promote, he will pitch your projects to editors for whom they are a fit and help you negotiate exclusivity. Publicists can also facilitate in-person introductions with editors, get you on the guest list of high-profile events, and broker introductions to show house organizers or their trade clients who could end up as licensees.

If you have a product line or publish a book, you will definitely need a publicist on your team. Many publicists work with designers on a project basis for the launch of a book, and it's a worthy investment, especially if you're targeting markets nationwide. Think about all of the media outlets in your city—radio, online, newspaper, and niche local. Now multiply those outlets by every city your line will be carried in. That's a lot of pitching! Hire a professional to do it.

What to Do with the Press You Get

Once you get some press, the first thing you need to do is thank the editor. At least send them an email, but I prefer a handwritten note and perhaps a small gift. As for your feature, share it. Tweet it. Post it on Facebook, LinkedIn, Pinterest, Instagram, or any other place you have an online presence. Don't forget to tag the publication and the editor. Send an email to the key vendors you used and ask them to share it with their clients and across social media. Include a link to the article in your newsletter and send it out to your list. If you're interested in building a relationship with a builder or architect, consider sending a copy along with a note of introduction. For at least a month following publication, include a short link to the article in your email signature. Finally, add a thumbnail of the magazine cover to the press page on your website, or a high-resolution version of the logo if it's digital.

Look for quotable copy. For example, did the writer speak about your approach to the room or describe your talent in a way you like? Were you included in a list like the "AD100," "Next Wave," or the "New Trad Designers"? Why not add that to a prominent place in your bio or as a tagline in your marketing copy? Highlight quotes you can use when you create your next postcard, Facebook header, or other promotional materials.

One of the most common fears I hear from designers who get published is that people will think they are full of themselves. As we discussed in chapter 3, what other people think of the fact that you've been published is not your business. Your business is to be in service at the highest level you can be throughout the course of your career, and getting published is a core component of career longevity. Remember, when it comes to people talking about you, they probably already do.

> "I will never give myself the
> luxury of thinking I've made it."
> —Zaha Hadid

Not All Press Is Good Press

Take the time to cultivate your image carefully. Often in the rush to be seen, designers often forget that the fastest way to get the media to notice you is to actually have something to say. Being press-worthy is about knowing who you are, how you want to impact the industry, being articulate, and having a take on the world. If you continue to evolve, editors will seek you out to hear your point of view.

Just because a publication wants to cover you—and there are many blogs hunting for new material daily—doesn't mean you should say yes. Use discretion. For the most part, what goes online stays online unless you have a lawyer intervene. Does what that publication stands for align with your own brand? Is it well written with quality photography? Who is the audience? For example, if you're working on building a reputation as a luxury firm, why would you allow yourself to be covered by a publication offering readers budget-friendly design tips?

Getting press and the visibility and recognition that comes along with it is a cause for celebration, but also an invitation to set boundaries for the way you want to be seen in our increasingly cyber world. If you don't, others can set them for you. Set up a Google alert with your name and company name to track the footprint you're leaving online. Add a disclaimer to the footer of your homepage next to the copyright symbol and in the portfolio section that tells visitors your images cannot be used without your permission. Why? Because some online writers, and the occasional desperado decorette, can drop them into an off-brand story, or claim your work as their own with an easy right-click and save. If you can't get them to take it down, take legal action. They can't say you didn't warn them.

Rose Tarlow's Point of View

Rose Tarlow is an antiquaire, designer, author, and creator of wallpapers, furniture, fabrics, and anything that will add to the everyday luxury of living. *New Yorker* architecture critic Paul Goldberger described her as a woman who is "unshakably sure of her own mind." She "balances emotion and intellect as well as any designer now living . . . her rooms [combine] sensual pleasures with geometric rigor, and every one of them is simultaneously a lesson in design and a lesson in living."[2] She opened R. Tarlow Antiques on Melrose Avenue in 1976 with an inventory of antiques from the Paris flea markets.

By 1979 the company, renamed Rose Tarlow Melrose House, had become a preeminent producer of furniture, pieces with charm and a textured story that seemed to flow from the proprietor herself. Tarlow traveled the world to find the most exquisite antiques from exclusive sources for her shop and her private clients, looking for the one piece in each shipment that would give character to the whole collection—one piece with such singular style that it could inspire a room. When she began designing her own furniture a few years later, she sought to create a collection where every piece was that special piece. In 1997, she was inspired to create her own line of textiles to complement her furniture. The fabrics range from sheers to velvets and include outdoor textiles. This comprehensive collection now includes proprietary leathers, trims, and wall coverings.

@MEBYDESIGNTV:
What do you think of the word brand?

@ROSETARLOW:
I don't like the word brand.

@MEBYDESIGNTV:
[Laughs] You don't like the word brand?

@ROSETARLOW:
It's something I don't want to have my name connected to. You go to meetings and everyone talks about brand, brand, brand. I don't like it. I don't want to be a brand. I want to be an individual.

@MEBYDESIGNTV:
Is there an experience you want people to have when they come in contact with your work?

@ROSETARLOW:
Yes, I just want them to think it's different. It's unique. It's not a thing that I've created to make my name. It's just what I do.

@MEBYDESIGNTV:
It's about personal expression then?

@ROSETARLOW:
Yes, brand sounds too generic for me.

@MEBYDESIGNTV:
Has press helped the growth of your business?

I've never really been somebody that looked for press. I think it's cumulative, all the things that go into it. I was fortunate because I was early, doing things before other people did them, like making the reproductions and the furniture. I was always in the first group, and the first group is always the one that's remembered. When I wrote my book, it was helpful because then you know they did all kinds of stories, and that was fun. It was a wonderful experience.

Writing the book?

I'm more proud of writing that book than anything because it was so difficult. I loved writing it and I would love to do it again, but you know, you have to be in the mood for it.

Yes, I know [laughs].

I didn't like the way it came out, probably because I had to relinquish control. But just writing it was rewarding, because I'm not a writer.

The Private House
Rose Tarlow

@MEBYDESIGNTV:
Do you consider yourself a visual person then?

@ROSETARLOW:
Yes, completely visual.

@MEBYDESIGNTV:
In the book, you mention a special form of discernment that's key to your creativity and success. How do you cultivate it?

@ROSETARLOW:
I was born with it. I knew even as a young person. I could tell when something was wrong. I can tell when something is wrong and I can fix it, but not always.

@MEBYDESIGNTV:
How does this discernment affect the way you run your business?

It's everything. When I make a piece of furniture, I can tell when it's off. Like with my cabinet maker, when we first started making furniture, he didn't speak English very well and he shook his fists and said in Italian, "What's the big deal? What's the big deal with an eighth of an inch? Why go bananas over an eighth of an inch?" That's the truth. I do that. I know it's wrong and I don't know how to fix it at that moment, so I just drop it and come back, and it always works out.

What sparked your decision to go from antiques dealer to reproduction designer?

The antiques weren't profitable at all, just a passion and a love. Because every time you sell something, you have to buy something else. It's not

Below: Rose Tarlow's Los Angeles Garden. Photo by Tim Street-Porter

a way of life if you want to live in a beautiful house and have great things, because you spend all your profit buying furniture. There was a time in my life that I did it. I was married and had time and then after a while, I couldn't keep the doors open. Los Angeles was not a place to sell fine antiques. I had no choice. It was very hard for me to start making furniture. I thought I was the worst person in the world.

@MEBYDESIGNTV:
Why?

@ROSETARLOW:
I was very young. Because I was such a dedicated antique dealer. I was so determined. Everything had to be perfect. I thought, "Oh my god, I'm selling out." Now it doesn't bother me at all, but I was very young.

@MEBYDESIGNTV:
How did you start your furniture business?

@ROSETARLOW:
People would say to me, "We bought eight dining chairs. You have six but we need eighteen." So I had all the cabinet makers that were restoring my pieces make them and it just developed that way. There was a beautiful shop next door available and I said, what could I put in there? It was more space to buy more antiques.

@MEBYDESIGNTV:
[Laughs]

@ROSETARLOW:
[Laughs] That was my passion. As a friend of mine said to me, "Telling Rose to stop buying is like telling a heroin addict to stop taking heroin."

@MEBYDESIGNTV:
[Laughs]

@ROSETARLOW:

When I was making furniture and designing furniture and fabrics, I would take one project at a time, sometimes because it was the only time I really had to buy anything without marking it up. I could still indulge my—you know what I love doing—which is what I've started to do again today."

@MEBYDESIGNTV:

Is that why you took such a small number of design projects?

@ROSETARLOW:

Yes, I took the projects mostly because I liked the people and because I wanted to buy things that I didn't have to resell. I love buying and seeing and finding.

@MEBYDESIGNTV:

You've been quoted as saying you don't love interior design.

@ROSETARLOW:

No, I don't like doing it. I don't like working for people.

@MEBYDESIGNTV:

How do you say no to people?

@ROSETARLOW:

I recommend them to other decorators. I don't even hesitate.

@MEBYDESIGNTV:

And it hasn't hurt you at all? I mean, in fact it actually makes you even more popular to say no, wouldn't you say?

@ROSETARLOW:

Absolutely. I think I'm more known for what I've turned down than what I've done.

@MEBYDESIGNTV:

[Laughs]

@ROSETARLOW:

It's the truth.

@MEBYDESIGNTV:

In terms of creating, do you have a schedule or are you more intuitive?

@ROSETARLOW:

I'm very intuitive. I work when I feel like it. I try to be more creative and spend time drawing and painting but I haven't recently, because I've been so busy since I bought my business back. I'm doing something new with it this time. I always like to reinvent myself.

@MEBYDESIGNTV:

Why did you sell your company, and then why did you buy it back?

@ROSETARLOW:

I sold it because I didn't like running a company. It was as successful as it could be. I'd been there such a long time and I didn't want to run people. I just didn't want to be in the shop anymore and I was very lucky because I sold the business a month before the crash.

@MEBYDESIGNTV:

Very lucky.

@ROSETARLOW:

Then the people who bought it really had a hard time. They put themselves in a big bind because they rented an expensive place they couldn't afford, which I still have to deal with. It was a bad time for them and they were going to sell to someone that I really didn't want to have it.

@MEBYDESIGNTV:

That's why you bought it back?

Twenty-seven people quit in one year. That was the year before I bought it back. Now I've brought quite a few people back and it's a challenge. I would never sell it again, ever. I would close it before I would sell it.

I love that you said you're trying to do something you've never done with it before.

I always try to do something new, to add something. First it was antiques, then it was fabrics . . . it has to be different this time.

You've had partnerships with Scalamandré and Bergdorf and other iconic brands. Would you do that again?

I wouldn't say that I would not do it. I'm doing something now that I want to put in department stores, little things, objects. I like creating things, and you have to have a place to put them.

[Laughs] You do. Did you expect your company would be successful?

Of course I did. When I was really young, a woman who was a very old decorator, a very good decorator, said to me, "I'm so happy for you. I never thought you'd make it work." And it never occurred to me that I wouldn't. That's what the key to success is. I just said, how long? How long is it going to take for me to be successful? It's the same thing here. It's really a mess that I've inherited. It's going to take a little while, but I have no doubt that it's going to be better than it was. If you have doubt, nothing works.

Do you measure success financially, emotionally, or both?

Both.

When you said it's going to be successful again, how do you define that?

It's going to be what I want it to be.

So your company growth has always been by feeling, not planned?

Yes. I'm not a businesswoman, and every time I say that in a meeting, people start to laugh.

[Laughs]

I'm not, but I have good instincts.

Why did you develop the Rose Tarlow Foundation for Women's Health at UCLA?

Because there were so many women who couldn't afford to get help. I'm also very involved with the David Geffen School of Medicine.

Do you think about it in terms of leadership or as something you must do?

Women's health is something that I like learning about and I think you should give back, and do. But do I want to go to meetings and sit there? No.

@MEBYDESIGNTV:

[Laughs] It seems like you have a team who does some of the stuff you don't want to do.

@ROSETARLOW:

I don't like the word team, either. That's my second least favorite word: team.

@MEBYDESIGNTV:

Oh. [Laughs] What word do you use?

@ROSETARLOW:

I just don't think team. But I guess team isn't as bad as brand. Team is kind of impersonal. Sounds like we're horses. I was in a big meeting the other day on the phone with the builder and architect for this project I'm doing. It was a big conference, ten or fifteen people, and he says, "We'll get your team." I said, "You know that I hate that word team." He says, "Yeah, you like a dictatorship, you don't like a team." [Laughs]

@MEBYDESIGNTV:

[Laughs]

@ROSETARLOW:

But no, it's fun to be back working, even though I never really stopped. It's fun to be creating things and doing things and building, having challenges to rebuild something. I like it. The last few years, when I sold the business, I took a few design jobs because I had to do something.

@MEBYDESIGNTV:

Like for Oprah? Come on, that's pretty fancy.

Springsteen, Oprah. I still collaborate with her. Everybody else is finished.

It's amazing for a woman who says no all the time.

I was doing a house for myself in Montecito near her and we got to know each other, and I just couldn't say no. You can't say no to that woman, when you meet her.

I loved reading your book because you talked about your childhood home. I could feel the house from your writing. That's what designers do best. Designers sell emotional experience and are transforming the energy of the room. It's not just the visual.

Absolutely.

It's not just the visual.

Yes, it's all completely energy.

People get so wrapped up in this business and the numbers and everything that they forget they're selling emotion, and that the biggest designers, you case in point, aren't selling the numbers, they're selling the emotion.

People are usually successful if they do what they love. People who don't like what they do are successful, but it's so much easier if you love doing something. I loved furniture and I studied furniture, but I didn't think I was going to open a shop. But my husband said, "My sister's coming into town and I've got to get a job for her. Why don't you open a shop, you have such good ideas?" So I did. I don't think I would have done it if he hadn't pushed me into it. It was the same thing with buying my shop back. I have a very close friend who said, "I'll do it with you. You have to do it." So I did. I don't think I would have done it if someone hadn't pushed me.

@MEBYDESIGNTV:
But you did it, and you're happy you did it?

@ROSETARLOW:
I really am. It's given me a new thing to do at this time in my life. It's a big challenge. When things come out right, it's when you're not thinking, when something subconscious works through you, when you let go of things. It's the same thing with decorating. I always think every room is going to be a disaster. But I know deep down that in the end, I'll make it better, and it always works if I keep moving. Like you keep writing even if it's not right. Just keep doing it.

@MEBYDESIGNTV:
Yes, I'm thinking about the letting go part. I think the letting go is so important. It's the key to receiving.

@ROSETARLOW:
It's trusting your experience.

@MEBYDESIGNTV:
I love that.

@ROSETARLOW:
I've learned to trust my experience of success. I know that it doesn't let me down.

Visit Rose Tarlow Melrose House in Los Angeles at 8540 Melrose Avenue; in New York at 979 3rd Avenue #1616; on Instagram and Facebook @RoseTarlowMelroseHouse; and on Twitter and Pinterest @RoseTarlow. The Rose Tarlow collection is carried at fine trade showrooms across the country. For more information, visit RoseTarlow.com

"My advice is to love what you do…to take one step at a time…work hard and to care about the people with whom you work. We live in a time of overnight fame that breeds the desire for instant gratification. This is not my story. I have worked almost every day for as long as I can remember. So my advice is to think small and see where it leads."
~ Barbara Barry

Audience Building 101

Have you ever had one of those moments when a random video shows up in your Facebook feed and when you click to watch, you discover 10 million people already did that, a year ago? Or you follow a RT back to a profile for an actress you've never heard of who has a following of a million plus or more. Don't despair. If you asked your non-industry friends if they like Vicente Wolf or Barbara Barry's work, most would be clueless. The good news is that your success isn't hinged on going viral. But you must find and engage *your* audience in the right way so that when they need an interior designer, hiring you is a no-brainer.

Engagement is the relationship you have with each person in your audience, and it's a word you'll hear repeatedly when it comes to tracking your online metrics. High levels of engagement help you create brand fame, generate sales through your services or product, and set up multiple channels for communication with past clients and new ones. The internet has given us powerful tools that can profoundly impact people's lives in a short amount of time, if you know how to use them.

As I said in chapter 4, engagement is less about building an audience of thousands than it is about building a tiny tribe you can influence. That's why it's so important to know exactly who your ideal client is and how they want to hear from you. Strategically planting seeds in places where your ideal client goes can reap miraculous benefits. You never know

Left: Interior by Barbara Barry. Photo by David Meredith

167

who is going to see your praise or when all of your efforts will unexpectedly convert a prospect. However, when you ask where your people are, add this important word: now.

> "An individual artist needs only a thousand true fans in her tribe. It's enough."
> —Seth Godin

If you'd told me a year and a half ago that your audience was a divorced bachelor, I would have said you'd probably find him on LinkedIn. As of the last quarter of 2014, I would add Pinterest. That's right. The online platform that most men didn't even know about at the start of 2013 saw 400 percent growth overall in 2014 and doubled the number of male users.[1] One-third of all signups came from men, with an equal split between male and female pinners in emerging markets like India, Korea, and Japan. Now more men use Pinterest in the US every month than read *Sports Illustrated* and *GQ* combined, and are pinning to boards like architecture, gardening, and fashion. However as of early 2016, that male user is starting to use Instagram where he can keep his feed private.

The point is that just because you figured out who your ideal client was last year doesn't mean his or her behavior hasn't changed.

Referrals

Up to eighty percent of an interior designer's business can come from referrals, so the easiest way to get new work is to ask clients to recommend you, whether by writing a testimonial for your website, forwarding your newsletter (you'll have one at the end of this chapter), or simply making a phone call or two on your behalf. Some clients might even offer to host a cocktail party to show off their home and introduce you to their circle of friends. You may consider incentivizing referrals by offering clients a gift certificate in exchange for their time, although if the relationship is a good one, most clients will be happy to help. The key is not to be embarrassed about the *ask*.

But what if the referrals I'm getting aren't ideal? What if you started out doing low-budget projects or color consultations and are ready to uplevel? Sometimes designers have a hard time saying no to friends of friends, especially if their client relationships are ongoing. In that case, make sure you have a formal intake process that creates separation between you and prospective clients. For example, respond to email or phone inquires with a short questionnaire that asks for budget and timeline details. If the answers don't meet your requirements, have your assistant make a call or respond to their query in a polite email.

If people aren't recommending you, get honest about the reasons why. Take a look at your client list; if the majority are happy customers who you enjoy doing business with, you must be doing something right. Some people will always find something to complain about, but if every client is a royal pain, you've got work to do. Ask yourself if you are operating at the high level of integrity and responsibility required for the work you do. If you've made a mess or a mistake, apologize and offer to clean it up.

The Opt-In

Capturing a visitor's email address is still the most effective way to convert a potential prospect into a client. Email is permission-based and allows you to communicate directly to your clients' inbox. It creates a higher level of trust in your communication.

You can capture email by including an opt-in or signup box in the top half of your website, which automatically directs visitors to a dedicated list organized in an email management program like Mailchimp or Awebber. This is different from an RSS (Really Simple Syndicated) feed. If you've been blogging for a while, you're probably familiar with this system, which sends readers an email blast when you have updates to your site. Although this used to be industry standard for updates, an email address is internet gold.

Your opt-in box copy will make website visitors an offer in exchange for their email address. For example, my client Holly Hickey Moore gives new subscribers a home maintenance guide. My client Tawna Allred offers tips on picking the perfect white. Whatever you've promised—and make sure it's something that will entice your ideal clients—when users enter their email, an auto-responder delivers the welcome gift immediately after they subscribe.

Many designers offer free reports like "Top 5 Most Costly Mistakes People Make During Renovations," or "Keep the Design Process Budget-Friendly." While a report like this may seem useful, it does not align with clients who are fearless about investing in the full value of your services. When you make budget-friendly design your value proposition, you're likely to attract clients who are worried about spending their dollars, and that usually makes your job harder.

Newsletters

If you don't have a steady stream of qualified prospects and a wait list, it's probably because you don't have a loyalty program for your clients and fans. Your email newsletter is the foundation of your loyalty program.

E-mail marketing works. Why? Because it's permission-based and according to every online marketing statistic, email is still the number one way for you to cultivate relationships with clients in every single kind of business and convert them into sales. When you've received permission and you're in touch in a way that is reliable, authentic, value-driven, and encourages action, you earn more.

Because here's the thing: if I'm the kind of client who can afford your services, I'm probably a busy professional who doesn't have a ton of time to spend on social. Even if I am constantly checking my phone, even if I pin for fun, I've probably only got time to check out my own feed or a tiny portion of the feeds of people I like. Will I remember to check yours? Will your post hit show up at the right time?

By comparison, as a professional in the twenty-first century, I always need to check my email. I'm also more likely to open email from someone I like—a.k.a. you—especially if I know your emails are worth reading. Because the underlying assumption is that when I subscribed to your newsletter, I signed up to be communicated with.

Even if I'm bad at checking email, even if I'm avoiding my inbox today, your message is still there waiting for me when I get back. Unlike your stream of social posts, your email doesn't just go away. And because email allows you to make unlimited contact, you are more likely to catch a potential client at time when they're ready to buy, one of the most important rules of sales.

Now, I'm not suggesting you give up your efforts on social media, because it's a key component of your seeding strategy. However, when it comes to building a tribe you can influence, your list will bring a bigger return. For example, when I started MeByDesign, before the business had that name, before I had a website or branded social media, I wrote a regular newsletter to a tiny list of just over 300 people and earned almost six figures in sales in my first year of business. I work with designers with several thousand followers on social media who haven't figured out how to convert those contacts into sales. Even designers who do convert on social see much greater returns when we add their loyalty program to the mix.

But you don't have to take my word for it. From purely a numbers perspective, email has nearly three times as many user accounts as Facebook and Twitter combined. That's a whopping 2.9 billion. In fact, Facebook and Twitter combined make up just 0.2 percent of the number of emails sent each day, not including spam.

A precedent has been set for customers to get offers and buy things through email. So they not only have a high tolerance for it, but they're actually more likely to be in a buying frame of mind. They're primed. On Facebook, they're ready to chat. On Instagram, they're escaping their day looking at pretty pictures. They may click to figure out where they can buy that sweater you're wearing, but a whole room? That's going to require a conversation. That's going to require them knowing what your process is and the value of your experience and expertise.

It strikes me that this is likely why so many people think design services are cheap. Are you cultivating an audience who thinks that designing a room is as easy as posting a picture?

If you have products and you don't have a newsletter, you are leaving money on the table. If you plan to write a book and you don't have a newsletter, you don't have the infrastructure to support the number one way authors guarantee and boost their sales.

In the vast majority of cases, business-minded people do not go to social media for private, one-to-one sales conversations, if they're serious. My readers often hit reply on my newsletters to engage with me. A few of those engagements will often lead to a sales call.

Even if you don't see results at first, you will if you invest the same level of care in your communication that you do in your business. Take a long-term view. When someone subscribes to your newsletter, they've signed up to be communicated with.

Create an editorial calendar with your ideal client in mind, mapping out twelve topics—one per month. That will give you a leg up when you sit down to write. If you don't like writing, assemble the images that will tell your stories visually. Distribute the newsletter on the same day each month, or quarterly at bare minimum. If you have products, consider bi-monthly or even weekly mailings with at least one solo-mailer exclusively devoted to telling product stories and winning sales.

If you're still struggling to find ideas for newsletter content, you're complicating things. If you've got your ideal clients right, they're your biggest fan, and because they care about you, they're interested in what you're up to. Use your newsletter to showcase projects in progress, community events you've participated in, and major transformations in your life and business, such as having a baby or hiring someone new on your team. Create a corner to post new testimonials or showcase publications where you've been featured, and to make special offers. Tell the story of the services you offer and the experience your design process offers them. Mirror the lifestyle your client aspires to in a way that shows your firm is not only their design solution but also their trusted friend.

If you're still struggling, listen more closely to the clues your audience is giving you. Was there a post on your Facebook feed that garnered discussion? Is a certain pin wildly popular and regularly shared? Is there an image that has been added to hundreds of ideabooks on Houzz. Write about it. Do you find yourself repeating certain information in your meetings or during the design process? Write about that! Sign off with an offer to book a consultation for a package of services or to offer to answer reader's questions. Whatever it is, give your audience a reason to get in touch.

Get Listed

One of the best things about being online is that if you plant the right seed once, your ideal clients can find you over and over again. Get your business listed on Google for free when you create a business page.

Google My Business makes sure your business shows up across Google in info, on Search, Maps, and Google+ so that customers can find you no matter what device they're using. In the last few years, Houzz has become a popular platform for bringing homeowners and home professionals together. It is searchable by state and profession, and many of my clients get fantastic leads from it. The key with any online listing is to make sure you're specific about who you are and whom you want to work with. If your minimum job is $50,000, $100,000, or $250,000, don't be afraid to say it. The same goes if you've listed yourself on other searchable sites like Yelp or Angie's List. You may get fewer leads, but they are more likely to be the right kind of leads.

One of the big complaints I hear about sites like Houzz, where DIY homeowner are among the users, is that people will ask for free advice— like a paint or tile choice. It is up to you whether or not to share the answer. Just because you are generous with your source this one time doesn't mean the person who asked the question will be able to achieve your result in their room. You can also respond that you give design advice in your complimentary newsletter and direct them to a sign-up URL. If they don't use it, it's there for somebody who will. However, if you choose not to answer, that's fine, too. But don't shift your energy negatively by giving them a lecture about what real designers do, or complaining about them in every Facebook group you're in. The more you focus on clients that aren't ideal, the more experience you will continue to have with them.

Get Off the Blog

If you write a blog and you started it after 2006–2008, when blogging was still new, don't assume that traffic will find it's way to your website without a push. With the rise of Pinterest and Instagram, there are many channels for visual creators to share their POV. Building your audience is going to require that you get off your own blog. The best way to do this is to cross-post your content on aggregate sites where the online traffic is greater than yours, or offer to guest post. When you guest post, you write exclusive content for another site that gives you a byline and links back to your own website.

The easiest way to figure out where to contribute is to make a list of the blogs you love to read. Next, consider which blogs your ideal client loves to read. If you don't know the answer, ask. Does the blog you want to write for share your audience and most importantly, what's in it for them? To get ideas, figure out which phrases and topics are trending on those sites. Is there something seasonal you can offer? If they have advertising guidelines listed, they also probably have an editorial calendar that will let you know how they've planned their content. What will your POV offer in service or to entertain their readers?

Length matters. Blogs, features, and segments have ideal lengths, depending on your audience's age, education, and geographic region. Make your title concise, snappy, and genius. Use grammar and punctuation correctly. Link back to previous, relevant blogs on your own site and make sure your bio includes a memorable one-sentence pitch about yourself, who you serve, and most importantly, your URL. When it comes to design, a picture is worth a thousand words, so select visuals that are beautifully executed for the story you want to tell.

To E-Design or Not to E-Design

In our digital world, virtual consultations using Skype, Facetime, and other video conferencing tools are expanding the places where designers can do business. If you're just getting started as a designer, working for a reputable e-design provider like Homepolish is a great way to get hands-on experience in the field, and marketing is done for you. But if offering virtual design or e-design is the only model for your design business, it may not prove as lucrative as you'd like in the short run. Why? Because these services are generally offered at a lower price point and clients will shop retail themselves, you'll have to sell a lot more packages to make a profit. Unless you plan to devote some serious efforts to list building, e-design may not be as easy as you think.

However, if you have a blog or a big online following, e-design is an excellent way to leverage it. If you're a national, premium design brand and you have product, e-design services are a targeted way to move it. Create design plans that include your products or product licensees. Windsor Smith's Room In A Box is an excellent example of this. The package has attracted celebrity clients like Gwyneth Paltrow and 1stDibs founder Michael Bruno.

The problem with a lot of e-design offerings, though, is that they come across as cheap, which won't work if you consider yourself a premium brand. Some e-commerce platforms even offer designer's services for free, with the incentive for designers being a commission on product sales—about fifteen percent. Again, when a designer makes cheap service their core value proposition, they're not laying a foundation for long-term growth.

As someone who has spent a lot of time behind and in front of the camera, I know that a webcam doesn't usually capture the energy in a room. Tilting the lens just an inch skews the perspective. Because so much of what a designer does is read, shift, and transform energy in a space, creating not only a stunning visual picture but an emotional response, e-design can be problematic. Maybe that's because I believe in the old adage, you get what you pay for or because I know the value of what an excellent interior designer means and as a professional, I'm willing to pay the price to work with one.

Channel You

Did you know that shoppers who view video are eighty-five percent more likely to purchase than viewers who do not?[2] Video captures your authenticity and is an instant vetting tool that shows your ideal client who you are and helps them decide in a few seconds whether or not they resonate with you. Video allows you to literally showcase how you want your company to be seen, and transparency is good for business. Video is also good for driving eyeballs to your home page. Having it on the landing page of your site makes your firm fifty percent more likely to show up on the first page of Google search results.[3]

In terms of online video distribution, YouTube is still the top of the funnel. It's the second largest search engine after Google. Think of YouTube as the online Walmart of your audience-building strategy. Consider this: Eight cents of every US dollar is spent at Walmart. In fact, $36 million is spent at Walmart every hour of every day.[4] Every minute, 300 hours of video is uploaded to YouTube.[5] In other words, YouTube is to video as Walmart is to America. But the shocking disconnect is that only nine percent of small businesses use YouTube, which means it's a huge opportunity.[6]

A proliferation of easy production tools has democratized content making. Good storytelling will always convert if your content is personally relevant, but you have to find your viewer on the right device at the right time. Is your ideal client watching television, watching videos on Facebook, or using their mobile device to do online research? If you don't know, ask or circle back to chapter 4 and get more clarity. Although internet marketing philosophy says any video will do, a sloppy talking head on a low-level web camera is definitely not on-brand for design. Unless, of course, you're building a DIY brand and a quirky, rough-around-the-edges approach is in harmony with what you want to create.

The story you tell needs to be well shot, well lit, and represent your aesthetic. Again, length matters. If you don't capture your audience's attention in the first eight seconds, they will go somewhere else. Until you have truly engaged your audience, the best online videos are short and to the point. You'd be amazed what a good storyteller can do with sixty to ninety seconds, or in three minutes for a webisode. Leave your audience wanting more.

Guest Television Spots & TV Hosting

If you think 90 million people watching HGTV is bad for the interior design profession, think again. Eighty percent of HGTV's audience is ready to hire you, so head back to chapter 4 to learn why you need to educate before you decorate. If you have an opportunity to make a guest appearance on a television show aligned with your brand, or on local morning news, go for it! Ask for a copy of the segment, upload it to YouTube, and link it to your site under a video or press tab. You can also include it as a widget on your blog.

If you want to be a television host, the first question to consider is your motive for being on TV. Is it because your POV is missing from the television landscape? Do you have a very different take on the design process? Or are you so outrageous that television audiences will instantly click with you? Think television is a quick ticket to big bucks? Not so much. Television shows take a lot of time to shoot, time spent away from your business. If you have a big team, it can work. But if your clients are used to seeing your face in meetings regularly, you have a lot to consider. Although television is still an effective way to build an audience and benefits designers with products to sell, it works best when the show and your network are on-brand with your design.

More and more these days, unless a show is based on discovering new talent, network executives take candidates' social following into account when they cast. If it comes down to a choice between two, the person with the larger social following is going to win. So if you want to be on TV, one of the most proactive things you can do is hone your voice online. Use YouTube to post short videos about what you do. At bare minimum, post a sizzle reel of your work to show producers and production executives exactly what they're going to get when they put you in front of the camera. Casting producers scour the internet for designers to feature as guests on serialized TV shows, and being a featured guest, or a recurring guest on an existing show, is a great way for audiences to get to know you. Morning news producers, especially, are on the hunt for compelling segments that they have to program 365 days per year, so make friends with an assignment editor now.

Understand, though, that the view of what entertainment is has changed dramatically. A generation of YouTube stars is skipping television altogether and using their followings and views to negotiate endorsement deals and product licenses. Twenty-five million broadband homes don't have traditional TV. YouTube captures more people in the eighteen- to forty-nine-year-old demographic on mobile than any cable network.[7] VOD, YouTube, and millennials have created an appointment-viewing ecosystem where videos can be screened directly to television. Media is being consumed where it wasn't before—on cellphones, laptops, iPad, watches, you name it—and brands that weren't considered entertainment brands are storytelling online. This trend, dubbed native advertising or content marketing, isn't going away anytime soon, so give deep thought to whether television is truly the best platform to reach your audience and grow your business.

Periscope & Snapchat

For the online camera host, social media apps are multiplying at lightning pace, and you must keep on top of the latest and greatest to find and engage your audience. Two hot ones are Periscope and Snapchat. Periscope is a live-streaming app that links with Twitter and has taken iPhone by storm, climbing steadily in app store rankings since February 2015. Periscope lets you stream a live video feed of whatever you're looking at or doing, a video selfie. Because it works in real time with Twitter, the comments on your feed will also be in real time, and you are instantly in conversation with your audience, literally broadcasting Channel You. When you use the app, a tweet is automatically posted to let your followers know that you are live, along with the link where they can watch and comment.

If you have teenagers, you probably know about Snapchat, which allows users (100 million) to send photos and videos that self-destruct. I'm way too paranoid to use an app like this, but Snapchat has introduced a feature called Snapchat Stories that allows you to assemble snippets you've taken over a twenty-four-hour period to create a montage of your day for sharing.

Both of these apps operate on the premise that time is fleeting. Periscope broadcasts are meant to be live, and the link to view each broadcast expires. Likewise, the Snapchat Story expires in twenty-four hours. Think of using apps like these as an opportunity to give your audience inside access into your world. Are you at the Louvre? Touring a celebrity home that is off limits to the public? Or do you want to send a message that is direct and personal? Even though using video seems like the height of visibility, these apps have an anonymous quality that appeals to the privacy-minded, especially with Snapchat because others must know your handle name to find you.

Paying for Social Currency

If you're impatient with organic growth, most social platforms offer paid advertising. Paid Facebook ads offer such specificity that you can target by age, income, city, or even favorite movie. Investing as little as $5 to add "likes" to your page or "boost" a post so that it appears higher in the newsfeed can be an effective strategy for clients with smaller lists and marketing budgets. Boosted posts can encourage page "likes" wherein potential clients can get to know you and opt in to your mailing list using the call-to-action or subscribe button once they're on your page. Twitter, Pinterest, and Instagram also allow users to create sponsored posts. Depending on your goals, these may be useful.

Remember, though, that the larger your following, the more responsibility you have to communicate with them. Five thousand "likes" on your Facebook page sounds sexy, but just because you bought them doesn't mean they will stay. Are you prepared to interact with that many people daily? The reason they "liked" your page in the first place was to build a relationship. If you're not willing to do that, you can bank on a high attrition rate or, worse, unmonitored comment-box conversations that veer off in a direction you don't like.

Managing Your Reputation

Even if you want to stay local, engagement is an important measurement of your communication's impact. Retweets, comments, shares, and subscribes are a sign that you've connected with somebody's emotions. When you share, the currency exchanged is trust. According to a study by the *New York Times* Insights Group on "The Psychology of Sharing," ninety-four percent of people carefully consider how the information they share will be useful to the recipient. We share to bring value to others, to define ourselves, to grow and nourish our relationships, for self-fulfillment, and to get out the word about brands and causes important to us. Seventy-eight percent share information online because it lets them connect to people they may not otherwise stay in touch with. A smaller but still significant percentage—sixty-eight percent—share to give people a better understanding of who they are and what they care about, and sixty-nine percent share because it allows them to feel involved in the world. On the receiving end, eighty-five percent of respondents say reading other people's responses helps them understand and process information and events as a citizen in our online world.

Even if they're not engaging directly in the comment box or with the like button on your online profiles, if someone is following you, chances are they are watching and listening to your interactions with other followers. When you misstep, they will strike back. Social media users will tell people if they loved your service but they will also talk if your service sucks. Don't be afraid to take on someone who is damaging your reputation online.

First, kill them with kindness, publicly. Although your audience may not always speak, it is watching. Is the criticism meaningful? Can you extract some truth and use it to tighten your policies and procedures and offer better service? Thank the person for the input and offer to do right by them, both publicly and in person with a phone call (my preferred method), or via email to set up time to speak in person. You're in a service business. Do what it takes to offer great service.

You may attract the occasional crazy person who will pollute your feeds with spam or say inappropriate things. Block them. The good news about most social media tools is that they offer ways to make you unavailable. I don't include my business address on my Twitter or Facebook profiles. I offer it by request to people I've screened.

Face-to-Face Still Counts

Planting all these seeds with social media doesn't absolve you from marketing the old-fashioned way. Face-to-face networking still counts. Shaking someone's hand and connecting with them in person is an important part of your Visibility Strategy. Be proactive. Many designers avoid networking because they see it as inauthentic, especially if they're on the introverted side. The relationships feel transactional. Networking may also require your participation in activities you think you don't have time for. However, if you can relate it back to the larger vision, it will get easier. Practice the one-sentence pitch you created until you can deliver it with ease, and don't worry about connecting with every person in the room. One meaningful conversation is worth more than a handful of business cards.

Attend an industry trade show at least once a quarter. Not only will you find inspiration, you'll stay up-to-date on products and procedures and meet a fellow designer or two. Solopreneurs can feel isolated, and industry events are a good place to find like-minded peers. Editors are almost always in attendance, and if you want to be published, this is your opportunity to let them put a face to a pitch.

Speaking to an audience of your potential ideal clients, and participation on industry panels are great ways to demonstrate leadership. Whether it's the Junior League, a private club, or a trade show, speaking gives people a first-hand experience of your offer. Many designers stop themselves from taking this leap because they don't have a presentation prepared. The fastest way to get one done is to book a date for a speaking engagement and make it happen. Use the speaking leads you generated with your STYLESheet™ in chapter 4. There is no better way to showcase your POV and hone the way you describe it. Presentations don't have to be lengthy. In fact, the best are usually interactive, with plenty of Q&A.

"Everything was controlled by Mrs. Knoll. Everything, everything the public saw—letterhead, business cards, stationery, graphics—it doesn't matter. She saw it and she approved and that maintained a very high level all the way through. In other words, she didn't have good design and lousy stationery, if you know what I mean."
—Murray Rothenberg, Knoll designer

Print This

Whether you're volunteering, attending charitable events, or speaking, keep your business card handy. When it comes to in-person networking, it's an extension of your first impression. Is it visually consistent with your brand, website, and social media profiles? What about the quality of paper it's printed on? If your contact information has changed, please don't hand out a card with a scratched-out address. Invest in a new one or take the card of the person you're being introduced to and send them a follow-up email.

On-brand printed support materials are also important. Do you have a welcome kit that you provide to clients after signing a contract? Is it on branded letterhead? Have you considered having your graphic designer create a branded folder? Some clients also print tote bags, pens, or a signature label that they can use to emboss white-label gifts to clients at the beginning or end of the project. I also recommend printing thank-you cards and sending them often.

A beautiful postcard featuring rooms you've designed is a great leave-behind at events or speaking engagements. Make sure the cards include your website, email address, and at least a one-sentence pitch about the services your firm offers so that you create the possibility of building your digital list, wherever you leave them. Do a quarterly or bi-annual mailing to give clients something tangible to post on their bulletin board or fridge. If you don't have a mailing list, consider doing a mail drop to targeted zip codes.

Is your firm working on new construction or a renovation for an extended period? Post a sign with your company name and URL on the property's lawn. Potential clients driving by will likely remember your

website address more easily than juggling their cell phone to snap a picture of your phone number.

Events

Consider hosting a holiday open house so people can experience a space you've designed. If your home isn't up to snuff, ask one of your clients to host, especially if it could benefit one of their charities. Are there seasonal or charitable events you can sponsor or decorate? For example, DIFFA—Design Industries Foundation Fighting Aids—is a multi-city event where some of the most talented and celebrated individuals in the worlds of fashion, interior design, art, and architecture come together to create spectacular, over-the-top dining environments. The event is covered by top-tier publications and the proceeds go to organizations that help fight HIV/AIDS.

If you've got product, why not organize a pop-up inside a favorite boutique or a high-traffic, empty retail location? Consider collaborating with visual artists, a local realtor, or a development company so you can reach more than one list. Events like these are also an excellent opportunity for local press.

Your Team = Brand Ambassadors

Marketing is no longer a discrete entity; it's deeply personal and extends throughout a firm to tap every function. Success comes not just from the team's ability to come up with a great idea, but also the leadership and culture inside a studio. Your team is representative of your brand whether or not you're there, so empower employees to make sales on your company's behalf. Whether or not you choose to incentivize these sales with commissions or spot bonuses, set the expectation that your team must be all hands on deck. That means inspiring them to work for a broader goal. Educate them on who your ideal client is and empower them to innovate your process. It doesn't mean they will take over and do things their way, but it does mean that you're open to their suggestions for incorporating technology and new practices that will allow you to stay nimble and grow.

Even small to mid-size firms can take a page from international giants like Gensler, the largest design firm in the nation whose work ranges from wine bottle labels to the Shanghai Tower in China. "Everyone at Gensler is a marketer. Everyone," says Robin Klehr Avia, regional managing principal and board chair at Gensler. gConnect, its in-house sales program, trains every practicing professional in the skills of client relationship management and marketing in a way that's congruent with the employee's personality and communication style—in other words, their own personal brand.[8]

"For employees to be entrepreneurial, they need to have a voice," says Avia, who joined Gensler in 1980 as a junior designer in commercial interiors—employee number twenty-four in the New York office—when the firm was just 300 employees. Thrown into a project manager role early on, she realized that leading teams came naturally.

Fred Schmidt, global corporate interiors practice chair at Perkins+Will in Chicago, agrees. "The people who come to work here or at any firm should be intrinsically in alignment with the mission, otherwise it's not going to be a great marriage," he says. What is the firm's stated mission and purpose? What's in the employee handbook, and how does that play out in day-to-day interactions and firm culture? Is what happens compatible with your core values? Employees who act like entrepreneurs inside large firms are rewarded with seniority, leadership, and employee bonuses.[9]

If you hire right, your team members will make your firm better and more financially secure not only by representing your brand but by creating new lines of business. For example, Tom Polucci, director of interiors at HOK's New York office, co-founded HOK Product Design, an independent spinoff that creates innovative products for the built environment.

"You can be your own little entrepreneur as a product designer inside HOK," says Polucci, who started out as a junior designer eighteen years ago in the company's St. Louis office. Designers are given a path to development and manufacturing and paid a percentage of royalties on products they create that make it to market. "There are lots of three-letter firms out there; a lot of us do the same thing," Polucci says. "How are we going to differentiate ourselves but also strengthen ourselves as a business and find better ways of doing things?"

Kelly Hoppen recently created Studio Hoppen, a separate studio to take on select projects run by four designers whom she trained over the years. "I didn't want people to come to Kelly Hoppen Interiors and not have me, so for thirty-nine years I designed every project," Hoppen says. "And I finally decided I couldn't do it any more."

Studio Hoppen works with the same architects and resources as the main office does, but without the A-list pricing they would pay for her personal involvement. The studio has a separate intake process, and the designers have the authority to operate independently so that Hoppen can expand other aspects of her business while continuing philanthropy and television work. However, she admits that she still checks in, because, ultimately, everything has her name on it.

Be a Good Citizen

Philanthropy and social responsibility are important pillars of leadership. At Gensler and HOK—two of the top five design firms in the US—good citizenship is part of the culture. Designers are encouraged to be part of something bigger than themselves.

For example, Gensler's gServe program, a grassroots effort led by many of the company's juniors, has helped to develop housing in India, a school in Haiti, and a New York city classroom, among other projects. "We're really into volunteering, making sure our people are out there helping in the community, because we're good citizens," Avia says.

HOK is the US Green Building Council's official design partner for Project Haiti, rebuilding an orphanage and children's center severely damaged in the 2010 earthquake. An all-volunteer HOK team, including architects, landscape architects, lighting designers, sustainable experts, and engineers at the senior and junior level committed themselves to the challenge of bringing highly sustainable design to developing countries. In Haiti, with no enforceable building codes or functioning infrastructure, the new net zero energy, water, and waste project meets LEED Platinum standards.

Your company's good works don't need to be massive in scale, but you do want to be passionate about community service. How can you use your skills to do something better for people? How can you build that service mentality into your culture? What charities are important to you and your team members? Do you donate a percentage of monthly sales to those causes? Will you sponsor a table at a high-profile charity event? Build a model for giving back. Making the investment to be a leader in your community always brings powerful returns.

Awards & Show Houses

Stop telling yourself that recognition doesn't matter. Awards build your brand's credibility by highlighting your standards of excellence and can positively impact your bottom line. Awards also boost your visibility among your peers. Add your email to design awards programs notification lists so that when submissions open, you're the first to know. When you win, let your clients know in a newsletter or send them a copy of the publication that featured your work.

Whether it's Kipp's Bay or the Dwell Home Tour, show houses also offer visibility and prestige. Since the ticket proceeds typically go to charity, designing a room in a show house is a great way to show leadership in your community. With participation comes the cost of construction and a time investment, but there is no better way for a large number of people to experience your work firsthand.

Remember, you don't need dozens of clients to be well paid. You just need to learn how to speak to a few of the right ones in an authentic way. The most important thing when it comes to audience building is the willingness to be wrong. You may have a gut feeling about a method or a topic, but when you put it in front of your audience, if it doesn't resonate, let it go. An even better idea is trying to get to you.

Barbara Barry on What Feels Beautiful

Born in California, Barbara Barry founded her eponymous firm in Los Angeles in 1985. It has grown to include residential and commercial design, along with lines of home furnishings with esteemed brand partners like Baker Furniture, Henredon, Kravet, Ann Sacks, Visual Comfort, and Kalista. Her audience is wide, and she has earned a distinctive place in design history with inclusion in *Interior Design*'s "Hall Of Fame," *Architectural Digest*'s "World's 100 Best Designers," and *House Beautiful*'s "Giants of Design." She lives unabashedly for beauty, both inner and outer, and sees them as intimately connected. Her work centers on living well on many levels, and she believes in engaging her clients' senses to offer them a visceral experience of the power of design.

@MEBYDESIGNTV:

You are self-taught. How did you find your way to interior design?

BARBARA BARRY:

My way into interior design was not a linear path, and yet felt like destiny having come from a family of talented women. When I dropped out of art school, I owned and designed a small cheese and wine store in northern California on the Mendocino coast. I believe it was quite charming and a few customers enlisted for my advice for their homes. One thing led to another and I finally moved to Los Angeles. It was only six months before I was on the cover of *Metropolitan Home*, the leading design magazine of the day. I never worked for anyone but myself and slowly began to get one client at a time. I never looked back. My success still seems like a miracle to me.

@MEBYDESIGNTV:
How do you define the essence of your brand? Is there an overall emotional experience you want people to have when they come into one of your rooms or use your products?

BARBARA BARRY:
Firstly I have to say that I love this question because it allows me to speak to "mood" which in the end is what beauty is all about. The experience I am searching for is calm, a calm respite in which to be nourished by beauty. Over the years I have thought a lot about what delivers that feeling. I have looked to nature with its subtle nuances and shadings and see it as my largest influence. Gazing out over the ocean with its infinite shades of blue relaxes me, gazing at a forest of green, the same feeling. I have brought this philosophy of subtle shading and the use of analogous color into my rooms to create calm. So the essence of my brand is a calm with a feminine essence.

@MEBYDESIGNTV:
You are an international design brand and leader, was the vision for your company's growth planned, or by-the-gut?

BARBARA BARRY:
Nothing was ever planned! Like I said my success was and is still a constant surprise to me but when I look back I can see that the partnerships I nurtured have led to long-term and fruitful relationships.

@MEBYDESIGNTV:
You've been very successful collaborating with iconic companies. Why did you decide to license? How can you tell when collaboration is a fit?

Right: Furnishing by Barbara Barry. Photo by David Meredith.

BARBARA BARRY:

When decorating I always created my own pieces with local craftsmen for my interior design clients. Once published, the attention of certain manufacturers came my way. Wanting to remain a designer versus a manufacturer I partnered with one and then another. I cherish the way a designer and manufacturer can find a good fit. In the end, design is the leader and they are the follower. We need each other. Almost all my licensee partnerships were and are a good fit. The few that weren't came at a time when the world was changing with the Internet.

@MEBYDESIGNTV:

When you talk about *Around Beauty*, you say the book you wrote is not the book you thought you would write, why is that?

BARBARA BARRY:

For years I had thought about doing a book of my work . . . both my interiors and my product but after waiting so long I felt the world just didn't need another book of interiors with descriptions. The desire to write more personally and to share my design principles by embedding them into short stories seemed right. I thoroughly enjoyed the process.

@MEBYDESIGNTV:

Describe one thing that has been critical to building the long-term success of your company.

BARBARA BARRY:

The people with whom I work have been crucial to my success. My clients, my employees, and my licensee partnerships; it is all about the people.

@MEBYDESIGNTV:

It is common for designers to become the face of their brands and you very much are. How did you become comfortable with that visibility? What do you think about the extra access that social media brings?

Right: Furnishing by Barbara Barry. Photo by David Meredith

BARBARA BARRY:
Actually I don't feel that I am the face of my brand, nor am I comfortable with that notion. I have spoken all over the world and have met thousands of people in service of the business but that was before social media exploded. Now I do the minimum and no longer make personal appearances, believing, or rather hoping, that good design will sell itself.

@MEBYDESIGNTV:
What one piece of advice would you give to designers who want to take their brands to the next level?

BARBARA BARRY:
My advice is to love what you do, take one step at a time, work hard, and care about the people with whom you work. We live in a time of overnight fame that breeds the desire for instant gratification. This is not

my story. I have worked almost every day for as long as I can remember. So my advice is to think small and see where it leads.

In terms of mindset/life balance, are there any practices or daily rituals you think are important to stay focused?

BARBARA BARRY:

Oh yes, throughout all, time balance remains one of the hardest things to achieve and the true measure of success. I balance my intense work schedule with time away in nature. I surround myself with beauty every day in as many ways as I am able. I find beauty renewing, uplifting, and energizing, and it gives me the energy I need to continue.

@MEBYDESIGNTV:

How would you complete the following sentence. Design is . . .

BARBARA BARRY:

. . . the most wonderful opportunity in the world. Everything can be a thing of beauty and should be because everything influences us whether we are aware if it or not. And sadly, the opposite is true too. Every manufacturer should enlist designers. I feel so privileged to have a life in service of beauty; it has brought deep meaning to my life.

Follow Barbara Barry on Instagram and Twitter @BarbaraBarryInc and on Facebook.com/BBarryInc.

"What's helped me significantly to reach our financial goals is licensing. It's something I really encourage other designers to do. Know who you are. Build a brand. Then go out and license it. Approach people. It's like sending your kids to school and college and then you cash in because they start sending money home."

~ Clodagh

Publishing, Licensing & Legalese

In 2000, I was in California for the first time, in Newport Beach where my cousin lived, and I got the idea for a line of T-shirts with words I liked embroidered on the front. American Apparel was just starting out, and I used its private label services to produce a line of T-shirts and underwear I called Girly Girl Bits. With a lot of stubborn hustle, I ended up selling that line in forty-four women's and gift boutiques. I didn't know anything about product sales, but by the end of a year, I had learned what to look for in a sales rep; that I hated inventory; why too many SKUs can be a bad thing; that all embroiderers are not created equal; and that cash flow worked best when cash flowed into my bank account instead of out. The internet was in its infancy, and if Etsy had been invented, there might be a different end to my story. Because that's the thing about launching a product line—it's a full-time job.

Product Power

Being creative means you're often flooded with ideas. If you've been in business for some time, you've probably created custom pieces for clients. You might think these pieces will naturally become part of your own line. For most designers, the creation part is easy, but what about the rest of it? Where will you have your prototype manufactured? What kind of minimums do you need to establish with your manufacturers to make this profitable? What about your distribution channels? What is your new-client acquisition cost? Is there a dedicated staff person on your team to handle orders? Do you have a marketing budget? How about a marketing plan? Do you have a following of rabid fans ready to click and buy? In other words, if you make it, how and to whom are you going to sell it?

Perhaps you're not worried about any of that because you plan to get a licensing deal with a well-known company. Fantastic! What's its incentive for partnering with you? Does your brand's name come with inherent value? Are you regularly featured in shelter publications, and do you have a solid body of press that illustrates you are editorial-worthy? Do you already sell a high volume of the company's products? No? Oh.

Now, I'm not saying your dream of having a line is impossible or that you should stop creating things, because if you're anything like me, you can't help yourself. But I am saying that the dream stage is a safe place to be. It doesn't require that you take action in ways that may stretch the boundaries of what you know. If making products is a true desire, you need to understand what it takes to make them a reality before you start spinning your wheels and your focus. If having a line is something you want, you need to build your support structure properly.

Crowdsourcing

If you decide to self-produce your products, build a prototype before you order a full run. For the right kind of product—tabletop or home tech—crowdsourcing is an interesting way to fund your development process. Collaborative websites like Kickstarter.com and Indiegogo.com are a huge opportunity because your audience gives you direct feedback on what they're willing to buy, while you retain ownership of your work. If people like your product, they can pledge money to make it happen. Kickstarter-funded art works have been exhibited at MoMA, the Kennedy Center, and the Smithsonian, among other places.[1]

When Fossflakes USA wanted to take its pillow to the consumer market, it set up a Kickstarter campaign asking for $5,000 within thirty days. Created by Danish inventor Lars Foss, the sleep pillow was inspired by snow and made with patented pillow technology. It was already a hit in the hotel industry and the company wanted to bring the products to consumers. In one day, 353 backers pledged $27,842. Not only did the campaign show that consumers were ready to buy, it also created some buzz in the process.[2]

If the idea of crowdfunding makes you nervous because you wonder how you will find people to pledge, that's exactly the point. When you launch your product, you will need buyers. Why not get the ball rolling before you invest a lot of money in something people aren't interested in and end up with inventory on your hands?

Digital Products

If you've developed a platform as a blogger, digital influencer, or speaker, or offer peer-to-peer education, you may want to create digital products for sale from your website. If your blog gets a decent amount of traffic, advertising a digital product above the fold is another way to earn income. Whether its a series of podcasts or a CEU, the market for digital products is big. It's also a passive income stream, but one that, for now, I don't recommend to designers at the high end of the market. Like e-decorating, if you don't get the positioning right, it can diminish the value of your brand because the price points are often low, anywhere from $9.99–$49.99. When you're selling fabrics at $300 per yard, it's a value disconnect. Earning money on the work you've already done, in perpetuity, sounds pretty good, but generating passive income with digital products also involves building a platform, a comprehensive marketing strategy including affiliates, and a whole lot of hustle.

Retail Roundup

Whether you're selling a physical or digital product, getting it to market is a full-time job. For physical products, appoint a dedicated team member to focus on inside sales. Depending on the volume you want to sell, you may also hire an outside sales rep. If you've got inventory and can handle order fulfillment, build a branded online store. Most Wordpress themes come with an e-commerce add-on, but you can also use a solution like WooCommerce or Shopify to easily list your products and attach a virtual shopping cart for payment. You'll still have to drive traffic to your site, though, especially if you've got digital products, because you will have to sell more units to make money.

I'm a big fan of e-commerce portals that have a built-in audience, like Chairish and 1stDibs or even Viyet for designer pre-owed furniture. Each of these platforms also has a trade program. Link the store tab from your website to the online store page you've created, and now you've got a partner directing traffic back to your website. Again, fit is everything, so choose one that is on-brand for your business. For better or worse, if a visitor happens to check out a product link, that product will be served to them in the Facebook Sponsored section as a preview, keeping your store top of mind.

If you have a brick and mortar store, you're not off the hook with online retail. Whether or not you choose to offer a curated selection of your merchandise online is your choice, but part of the job of owning a store is to build community. Do you have a dedicated Facebook page? Are you listed on Yelp and other online directories? Do you have a weekly newsletter highlighting your products and new arrivals? With flash sale websites and online retail in the mix, foot traffic will not be enough to sustain your business. Build a brand that becomes a go-to shopping destination and use all the online tools you can to get the word out.

Affiliate Programs

An affiliate marketing program lets brand partners, bloggers, and your fans help with online sales and drive traffic to your store. In brief, you provide them with a unique link to a product for sale. They include that link in a post or tweet that speaks about your product. If someone clicks on that product and then buys it, the affiliate gets a commission on the sale. Full disclosure is expected. For example, your affiliates' site should state that the affiliate may earn a commission on the purchase, at no cost to the buyer. It's a win/win that's relatively easy, though only one to two percent of readers click through, so you'll need a high volume of traffic.

Because affiliate marketing is transactional in nature and there is financial incentive for people to sell your products, be selective about partnerships. Make sure the company selling your products is the kind of company you want to do business with, and that the site they're selling your products on looks and feels like you. Here again, a large number of affiliates may be sexy, but the key is finding the right sites to deliver consistent conversions.

Why License?

Licensing is one of the most important ways interior designers can build brand awareness and create passive income. It's a non-traditional business partnership that allows companies with different kinds of expertise to partner for profit. The brand or licensor rents its essence—emotional, spiritual, aesthetic—to a manufacturing partner (the licensee) to offer products and/or areas of service that the brand doesn't offer. With the right fit, licensing is low-risk, profit rich, and big business. In fact, design and art properties generate more than $9 billion in sales annually, and licensed furniture revenues now approach $5 billion, roughly ten percent of the US design industry.[3]

"The world is changing a lot, and you're going to hear the word lifestyles over and over again," says Ellie Altshuler, an attorney who specializes in licensing and intellectual property at Nixon Peabody in Los Angeles.

Plan & Prepare

Find Your Fit

Negotiate

Develop

Produce

Distribute

Market & Manage

Report

Altshuler negotiates, drafts, and handles licensing deals in a multitude of categories, including home décor, paper goods, apparel accessories, and mobile applications. She's also dealt with celebrity valuations involving high-profile dissolutions and infringement. "The most important thing when you're launching a brand is to know who your target buyer is," she says. "You want to identify, even from the details of age, gender, and price point, what their life looks like, because if you're going to expand into licensing, you want to hit more than one area in which they'll be buying goods."[4]

Depending on the product category, licensing gives a brand the opportunity to expand its offering to a new market or reach the same audience at a new price point. Large clothing companies like Zara, which have home stores in Europe, or H&M, which sponsors Coachella, are moving their fashion brands into related products and categories like home goods, music, and entertainment. At Maison Objet, held for the first time in Miami in May 2015, Roberto Cavalli introduced a line of luxury bedding to the US. In April 2015, home company Serena and Lily introduced a fashion line.

Unless you're the Olsen twins, who went up-market when their mass-market children's brand Dualstar morphed into The Row, start exclusive before you tap into audiences at lower price points. Good examples of this are Target's collaboration with designers like the late Michael Graves, DwellStudio, and Nate Berkus. When you license, your brand officially becomes a living entity that can continue even after you've passed on. The brand is now bigger than just the goods you're selling. Think of Rose Cumming or Angelo Donghia, legacy products that embody the designers' vision.

Plenty of celebrities inhabit the interior design licensing space—Ellen DeGeneres, Brad Pitt, and Lionel Ritchie, to name a few. Despite this, the market isn't as crowded with "stars" as you might think, and you don't have to be a celebrity to be a licensed brand. Sure, some large companies bring in celebrities to launch home lines, but to-the-trade licensees partner with interior designers who they know and who are known by their peers. In identifying a trade partner, figure out what's missing in their offering. What insights do you have about their audience? Have any of the projects you've published featured their products? Keep in mind, too, that unless your design is a runaway hit, you'll have to do your part to sell it. Your trade partner won't continue to offer what doesn't sell.

"I've been doing licensing for twenty-seven years and it was something that was done sort of on purpose at a time where people really weren't doing licensing that much. It started in a very funny way. I was traveling through Thailand and I came up with some designs for flatware and I had them made and started selling them, and then produced china and started selling that. Then from that, it became very successful, and from that, companies started to come, like a company that's no longer around called Sasaki, and they did china and flatware. So I just started designing flatware for them. Niedermier, I've been doing for the last twenty-four years, carpeting. Baccarat. It came about sort of by chance, and some have worked out and some have not worked out. Because I think when you're doing product, it's a marriage and sometimes marriages don't work. You know, of your expectations for the quality, and their expectations for sales. It's a very sort of touchy thing."

~ Vincente Wolf

As with all business marriages, it's important that you don't jump into this serious commitment without someone to negotiate the terms on your behalf. When the late Michael Graves spoke at Dwell on Design a few years back, he said one of the biggest mistakes he made was negotiating his own agreement for the Alessi kettle. Turns out that iconic object earned him very little. The financial risk is weighted heavily in favor of the licensee— the manufacturer—which means the brand owner will probably have to give up more control than she is used to. Hire a lawyer who specializes in trademark and licensing and has a proven track record.

Whether an interior designer and a manufacturer partner to increase brand awareness or move the conversation in a different direction, the collaborations are purposeful and work best when they're symbiotic. If you don't value how a potential partner's product is made, or the company's communication style, why would you want to be associated with it? If you're aiming for longevity in your business, don't rush to partner with a brand unless it's a true fit. Because when you partner with companies that you love, it's a win/win for both of you.

Your Namesake

Many design brand names are eponymous: Vicente Wolf, Barbara Barry, Kelly Hoppen. Other designers create stand-alone brand names for their products and add their own name as a description in the marketing. For example, Shabby Chic by Rachel Ashwell, or Jasper by Michael Smith. If your name has independent value, consider that during the licensing negotiation process, because it can complicate things if you decide to sell your company to a larger holding company later.

It's not uncommon for fashion houses to go on without their namesake, as did Dior, Givenchy, Oscar de la Renta, Calvin Klein, and Donna Karan. In June 2015, Karan, the sixty-six-year-old founder and chief of Donna Karan International, stepped down from her company after reports that her relationship with LVMH Moët Hennessy Louis Vuitton, the French conglomerate that bought the house in 2001, had deteriorated. Her collection was suspended, and new designers at the helm focused their efforts on DKNY, a brand she also created.[5] Although you may have created a legacy company, selling your brand means not only selling your vision and your name, but also its legal use.

Brand Partnerships

Brands work with design influencers for different goals, but mostly because the designer has a POV and/or audience that is synergistic with his own. As social media influencers raise the bar on what it means to engage with an audience, brands need to find new ways to reach these viewers and provide the constant interaction and genuine connection they expect.

Sometimes, though, brands want to change the direction of the conversation around their product or offer, and so they partner with an unexpected influencer to help communicate that change. Either way, the collaborations are purposeful and work best when they're symbiotic. Brands (and/or their agencies) and creators must work together to create content with a shared purpose that can lead to deeper relationships with the creator's fans.

If you don't value how a company makes its products or its communication or marketing style, why would you want to be associated with it? If you're aiming for longevity in your business, don't rush to partner with a brand unless it's a true fit. Because when you partner with companies that you love, it's a win/win for both of you.

If you are paid to write about a product, or a company gives you its merchandise in exchange for a blog post, the Federal Trade Commission (FTC) requires that you let your audience know. The same consumer protection laws that apply to commercial activities in other media apply online, especially in the mobile marketplace. These laws vary by state, and it is the publisher's responsibility to know what they are.[6]

Posts about gifted merchandise or posts that you were paid to make must include the words "sponsored post" or similar language, positioned as closely as possible to the item you're promoting, regardless of the online platform. So that may require you to format the position of the language differently for desktop and mobile phones. If you share your post on social media, you have to include the disclosure in the copy along with the post's link, or, in the case of Instagram or Pinterest, the image. Why? Because not everyone who sees your share is going to click on that link and see the sponsorship disclosure on your blog.

If an appliance company takes you on an all-expenses-paid trip that you're talking about on social media, you are endorsing the brand, and in the FTC's eyes, that counts as an advertisement, too. Ask the company's publicist or legal team for the language they'd like you to use. Those affiliate links I spoke about earlier must also include a disclaimer on every single post. Like everything else in the online world, these rules are changing rapidly. Check ftc.gov for current guidelines.

Agents vs. Lawyers

One of the easiest ways to distinguish between lawyers and agents is that lawyers are paid up front per negotiation, and agents are paid a percentage of your earnings or royalty on the proceeds of your sales in perpetuity. Depending on the stage of your business, you may need one or both on your team. Like photographers, lawyers specialize. You may have a contract lawyer and a lawyer who specializes in licensing and intellectual property.

As a producer, I negotiate licenses and terms of agreement for television and the ancillary products associated with them, but when I wrote this book, I signed with a literary agent who has a long track record in publishing. She knew to ask for things unique to publishing that I hadn't even thought of. As the industry grows, people who call themselves design "agents" are popping up all over the place, but it's a tricky distinction because the industry isn't regulated. Know this: if someone is calling himself an agent, you shouldn't be paying him up front. That's a consultant, and those services are different. Whether or not you pay a royalty for the creative material someone licenses on your behalf is your choice, but it might be a costly one, so do your research.

Style Guides

Your style guide, brand guide, or brand book is the bible when it comes to you, your brand, and the products you design. It is the single most valuable sales and marketing tool a designer can have to drive good deals. It also helps the licensee's sales team create a path for your products to market. A style guide shows how to consistently communicate your brand's vision. It communicates your brand's promise, mission, values, history, and sometimes anecdotal stories about the brand. It provides product descriptions and sets the expectation for how they will be delivered. It includes practical assets like design plans in every phase, concept boards, product specifications, logo, typeface, and Pantones. Depending on the depth of vision and the category, it can also include label design, hangtags, signage, and other point-of-sale tools. It includes your media publication history and relevant market research, and may also include supplementary marketing tools like video. Like all of the pieces of your Visibility Strategy, invest what it takes to get your image right. Work with people who specialize in the creation of style guides and related materials. They will ask questions and include things you wouldn't have thought of, because they do it all the time.

Folio

Publishing is another way of extending your brand. Books are the physical expression of a designer's POV. Titles like Vicente Wolf's *The Four Elements of Design*, *Martyn Lawrence Bullard: Design and Decoration*, and Barbara Barry's *Around Beauty* are testaments to each designer's style. Although royalties on books aren't huge, there is a prestige factor with folios that creates awareness and opportunities for access to international clients, press, and products.

Books are usually the culmination of many years of achievement. The designer has blazed new ground and has something to say. Good publishers are not interested in helping you to check a box on your marketing list. A book is a large investment for a publisher, and its also the legacy and expression of your creative mind. Every publisher has its own brand and point of view regarding the selection of titles. Do your research before you submit. Unless you have a relationship at a well-known publishing house, work with an agent who can help you negotiate the finer points in your deal. For example, how much input will you have into page layout and cover design? How long will your book be on the shelves? Know the publisher's magic sales number. If you sell 7,500–15,000 copies of your book, you'll probably get the opportunity to do another one.

A book proposal is the selling tool for a nonfiction book and will include, among other things, a sample chapter, table of contents, and, of course, a selection of spectacular photography. If words aren't your strength, consider hiring a writer who gets your voice to collaborate on the text. Ask someone with name recognition who adores your work to write the foreword. Publishing a book is an expensive proposition, but less so if you've been archiving your work. Start investing in photography early so when the time comes, you're not photographing from scratch. You will also be a partner in marketing. Whether it's book signings, parties, speaking engagements, or distributing review copies to relevant press and online influencers, you will share and likely shoulder the responsibility of getting the word out.

Self-Publishing/Custom Publishing

Just as the internet has disrupted the design industry, it's also disrupted the publishing industry. According to *Publisher's Weekly*, self-published books now represent thirty-one percent of e-book sales on Amazon's Kindle store. Because self-publishing is less expensive than traditional publishing and the quality control isn't as stringent, self-published authors dominate only in genres like sci-fi/fantasy, mystery/thriller, and romance.[7] When it comes to design, coffee table books by established publishers still rule.

Some designers think that if they custom-publish a book, it will boost their firm's brand value. That's fine if you're simply looking for a thank-you gift for clients. But if you're trying to build credibility with shelter publication editors, traditional publishing is the way to go. Custom publishing is the equivalent of paid advertorial but without the built-in audience and long shelf life that traditional publishing offers. Although a self-published book can help you build a platform, it doesn't come with guaranteed distribution or recognition. When a book comes through traditional publishing channels— agent, acquisitions editor, and editorial committee—it's been vetted and refined multiple times. There is a qualified group who believes in the relevance and value of the work. Unless you have a thriving platform or the sales numbers to back it up, it may be tricky to get editorial coverage for your self-published book in mainstream media.

However, if you've built a platform as a speaker, design blogger, and/or YouTube personality, and you have a built-in fan base, by all means self-publish. It will be more lucrative. Create an on-demand version using the self-publishing tools of a well- known book commerce site like Amazon, and then use your newsletters and online channels to sell directly to your audience.

Legalese

None of what is written below should be construed as legal advice, but it outlines the broad strokes so you know what to ask about when you speak with an attorney.

Copyright, Trademarks & Patents

To differentiate yourself within your category, it's important to have a strong brand identity. Your headshot and/or logo must immediately indicate what you stand for and that is the foundation of your intellectual property. A trademark, legally indicated by the symbol TM, is any name, symbol, figure, letter, word, or mark used by manufacturers or merchants to distinguish their goods from others. It shows ownership and is usually registered with the Patent and Trademark Office. Trademarking identifies you to your customer as the source of products and protects your brand so that nobody else can use your name within that category.

Just because you own the URL does not mean you own the trademark. That said, here are some DIY basics. When you register a trademark, think about two things. First, where are you selling the goods? Next, what category are you selling them in? For example, if you want to sell fabric, books, and fragrance with your brand, those are three different categories and you will have to register your trademark in each one. As you decide where you're going to license and in which areas you want to grow, make sure that you have your trademark registered in each category so you have protection there, too.

Copyright protects the art work itself and is particularly important when it comes to publishing and textiles. For example, if the textile pattern you design becomes an iconic one, like the work of Scalamandré or

Designers Guild, and a clothing manufacturer wants to license it for use on a skirt, you own the copyright and can profit. It's the fixed representation of your idea that needs protection; ideas themselves don't have copyright protection. If you're self-publishing, register your book with the US Copyright Office.

Protecting furniture design is difficult under US law. Copyrights protect only "conceptually separable ornamental designs on furniture," not the overall design. Makers of iconic furniture pieces usually rely on "trade dress" registrations with the Patent and Trademark Office to discourage copycats. Recently we've seen a lot of midcentury designs knocked off, but there is a pretty good argument that designers' trade dress rights don't apply because nobody has taken action for many, many years.[8] Design patents take an average of fourteen months from filing to approval and expire after fourteen years. A company must also show that someone will be able to identify the maker of the product by the design. When it comes to copyright, patent, and trademark protection, your best investment is to hire an attorney who specializes in this complicated and ever-changing area of expertise.

Terms & Conditions

The terms and conditions page of your website lays out the rules for strangers who come to visit. These pages can limit your liability should a customer take you to court, as well as protect your rights with respect to the information you share about yourself on your website. Considering a court will look at your website terms to determine the contractual terms between you and the customer, do the work to make sure this page holds up in court. Again, consult with a lawyer, or if you're just starting out, use an online terms and conditions generator.

Include a disclaimer stating that you can't be held responsible for errors in web content and that, to your knowledge, the information provided is accurate and complete. If you allow visitors to post comments, the disclaimer must limit your liability in the event their posts are offensive.

Copyright and trademark notices are key because you are collecting email addresses—at least you'd better be after reading chapter 7. Put a privacy policy in place that complies with the Privacy Act and lets visitors know that you are collecting email addresses and you won't share those with third parties.[9] If you don't want people to use your photography without letting you know about it, say so. I would also recommend you put this request somewhere on your portfolio page and state that if someone does use your work, they must give you credit.

Fair Use

The right to free speech is constitutional, as is ownership of copyright. These tenets encourage creators to make new work. Under the 175-year-old fair-use doctrine, copyrighted material like your portfolio photography and blog posts may be used by other people, without compensation if it's for purposes of criticism, comment, news reporting, teaching, scholarship, or research. It's often cited among documentary filmmakers, who use large volumes of clips to tell their stories without having to pay hefty licensing release fees.

This same law applies to the internet. Some bloggers citing "fair use" will grab your images to use in producing their own blog content and Instagram posts, whether or not they are synergistic with your own. Is that legal? It depends. Free speech trumps private property when the new work is in the public interest, but there is a gray area in terms of what that means.

According to Michael C. Donaldson, a Los Angeles entertainment lawyer and copyright law expert, chances are it will be considered legal if the blogger can answer yes to the following questions: Does the asset illustrate or support a point you're already making in your new work? Do you only use as much as is reasonably appropriate? Is the connection between what you're using and the point you're making clear to the average reader? If not, you can go after them to take it down or demand a licensing fee.

Creative Commons

Creative Commons (CC) is a nonprofit organization that develops, supports, and stewards legal and technical infrastructure to maximize digital sharing. Copyright was created long before the emergence of the internet, and actions we take for granted like copy, paste, edit source, post, and share aren't always legal. The default setting of copyright law requires all of these actions to have explicit permission, granted in advance, whether you're an artist, teacher, scientist, librarian, policymaker, or just a regular user. To achieve the vision of universal access, CC provides a free, public, and standardized infrastructure that creates a balance between the reality of the internet and the reality of copyright laws.[10]

CC offers free, easy-to-use copyright licenses that provide a simple, standardized way to give the public permission to share and use your creative work—on conditions of your choice. For example, you may want people to share your work as long as it's for non-commercial use. In this case, a CC license lets you easily change your copyright terms from the default of "all rights reserved" to "some rights reserved." Creative Commons licenses are not an alternative to copyright. They work alongside copyright and enable you to modify your copyright terms to best suit your needs.

If you're a blogger and want people to share your work widely, using a CC license is amazing and an easy way to share. The same goes for your portfolio, but check with your photographer to make sure you've got the appropriate rights.

E&O

In the entertainment business, errors & omission insurance is de rigeur because it protects your business, and in some cases your personal assets, from professional liability that stems from your design work. Policies provide protection against an error in the materials used, the failure to obtain a client's consent to change the design or materials, or misinterpreted advice that could lead your client to take financial action against your business. These types of policies also usually cover you against bodily injury as a result of your professional services, failure to deliver a project on time, and client allegations related to your completed work. Make sure your policy includes independent contractors working on your behalf and provides coverage for legal defense expenses.

How to Deal with Copycats

Imitation is the sincerest form of flattery, or so the saying goes, and copycats are par for the course when you're successful in creative business. It's an increasing problem on the internet where business has gone global and foreign poachers serve up stolen copy in other languages that can be hard to track. The good news is that closer to home, a well-defined brand can make the internet a lot smaller.

One of my clients had her office design ripped off by a fellow blogger. The blogger published photos of my client's office and passed it off as her own project. Luckily, the design had been published, so the blogger was not as smart as she was nervy. In another case, someone hired one of my clients to design her first home and then started a blog and business claiming the work was entirely her own. In the first case, it was a fan of my client who discovered the copycat and took her to task. In the second case, a strongly-worded lawyer's letter resulted in the photos being taken down and the end of a friendship.

I'm a big believer that certain ideas pop into the zeitgeist because it's time, which is why it's common for more than one person to have the same idea at once. It's why Apple and IBM came onto the scene at the same time and why, as a story producer, I've received the same pitch idea from strangers on different sides of the country more than once. Some ideas get traction, earn media attention, become mainstream and create opportunity, and earn big bucks. Others don't, and that's where the trouble starts. Who knows how many people thought up personal computing devices, but only a few took action in the way that those now-ubiquitous brands did. From a legal standpoint, it's why ideas can't be copyrighted, but the expression of them can.

It's a slippery slope, because the foundation of learning is imitation. It's how as babies we learn to hold a spoon and how later as artists, we're taught the how-to of our craft. In the beginning, copying is a requirement of the creative process; so is inspiration. You'll often hear creative people say they were inspired by so-and-so when they made something. Being inspired by the work of another maker, artist, or designer is one of the most beautiful parts of the creative process. However, I often hear designers say, "You don't need to buy XYZ original. We'll do something custom and it will look exactly the same." Perhaps they would be less cavalier if someone was ripping off one of their furniture designs?

To me, the difference between a copycat and a pro is credit. Pros are generous with credit and give it when it's due. They've given up copying for something far greater: self-expression.

When it comes to copyright infringement, the Digital Millennium Copyright Act (DMCA) is a federal law that protects the integrity of copyright management information and guards against online copyright infringement. It outlines a formal process that creators can follow to enforce their rights and protect their content. The process for demanding removal of your content is informally known as a Takedown Notice. Sending the notice is the best way to protect your content and make someone stop using your stuff.[11]

Whether it's a blog, newsletter, tweet, or Facebook post, you control who can and cannot re-post your content. If someone uses it without your permission, send them a DMCA notice that demands they take it down. Although it's not a guarantee, it tells the infringer that you mean business. If that doesn't work, contact a lawyer for advice.

Karma

As for those inclined to copy, I get that you're not sure who you are yet and that's why you're trying everybody else's image on for size. But you can't get there following someone else's roadmap. First, because you don't know where it's going. Next, because you're driving another car. So take the shortcut to your success. Get to know you. Then, stop believing the lie that you have to be someone else to succeed. You are enough. So forget about copying someone else and start doing you.

If you've been copied, you may be tempted to keep your ideas underground or play a smaller game. It takes courage to be creative. You're doing the work and putting yourself out there, and as much as other people want to be like you, it is genetically impossible. Devoted fans want what you offer, not a copy. Use this STYLESheet™ to tighten your online protection game. Here are a few things you can do:

1. Does your website have Terms & Conditions listed? Would you prefer to use one of the templates that CreativeCommons.org makes available?

2. Watermark images of your work. Add the copyright symbol and your name—or preferably your URL—to every image that exists online. Also include copy on your website reminding visitors that none of the content may be used without your permission, and that there are consequences for ignoring your request.

3. Google yourself. Over the years, I've discovered articles I've written on the websites of well-meaning (I'm sure) folks who are using my content to help them pimp their services. I offer them two choices: pay for a use license or take it down.

4. Google your images at least quarterly. If you're using a Mac, drag the image from your site into the search box at http://images.google.com/. Google searches for your image and shows you the list of sites where that image is found. Using this method, one of my clients found her images on two overseas stock photography portals.

5. If you're using photographs of another designer's work in your blog or other online communication, have you given them credit? If not, fix that now.

Martyn Lawrence Bullard's Brand Fame

Martyn Lawrence Bullard is an award-winning interior designer and product designer, author, and television personality. His work has appeared in over 4,000 publications worldwide, and his projects are featured in more than ten coffee table books. Martyn's bestselling coffee table book, *Live, Love & Decorate* was released by Rizzoli in 2011 and his second book, *Design & Decoration*, was released earlier this year. Clientele include Tommy Hilfiger, Cher, Ellen Pompeo, Sharon and Ozzy Osbourne, Aaron Sorkin's home and executive offices at Warner Brothers and Paramount Studios, and many others. Although known mainly for his high-end residential design, he has also lent his talent to the commercial and hospitality sectors, designing the Colony Palms Hotel and Purple Palms restaurant in Palm Springs, Red O restaurant for master chef Rick Bayless, Castello Di Santa Eurasia in Umbria, and the historic Chateau Gutsch Hotel in Switzerland.

@MEBYDESIGNTV:

How did you get started in interior design?

@MARTYNBULLARD:

I have a very different story. I always call it my Hollywood story in reverse. Because, like everybody else in Hollywood, I came here to be an actor, to be a star. As with everybody else, you usually end up serving coffee in a coffee shop. [Laughs]

Left: Martyn Lawrence Bullard. Photo by Tim Street-Porter

So I had a very interesting journey with that for a few years. But I helped support myself by buying and selling little bits of antique jewelry and pottery and anything decorative that I could. Little did I know that I'd get cast in a movie where I played Eartha Kitt's boy toy. And from that movie I became really good friends with the producer. And the producer came to my little house that I sort of furnished out with all stuff from the flea markets. I had no money in those days, it was all done really on the cheap and they loved it. So they asked if I would do their offices, which were called the Hollywood Film Works. The day it was finished, the president of Capitol Records called me and said, "Will you come and do the Capitol building?" Which I thought, this is kind of crazy, is that the White House? [Laughs]

So a month into doing her project, she was getting married and again, in true Hollywood style, she ended up having me come and do the wedding because her wedding planner OD'd the day before the wedding. I'd never done a wedding before in my life and I went and bought loads of rose petals and kind of whipped up this crazy Moroccan-y thing in her house. At the wedding she sat me next to a lady called Cheryl Tiegs, who unbeknownst to me was this American icon, the world's first supermodel. And by the end of the wedding, Cheryl had hired me to do her house, which was pretty extraordinary, because at the time she'd gone through interviewing every major interior designer in the States. She hired me, no experience, no training, no anything, but we just kind

Below: Interior design by Martyn Lawrence Bullard. Photo by Douglas Friedman

of clicked. We finished the project and nine months later, it was on the cover of six magazines around the world. And I was declared a new LA design talent and the rest is kind of history.

@MEBYDESIGNTV:
So relationships are super important for your process then?

@MARTYNBULLARD:
In my process, a lot of it is very much about the relationship. I've had amazing clients. I've worked for people that I could only ever have dreamed of working for. And it's been incredible because a lot of those relationships have really turned into amazing friendships and I'm on

to their fourth house. I've watched their kids grow up—well, that's making me sound old—but it's about the real integral relationship. When you have that with a client, you end up coming up with really beautiful, really individual projects, and that's what my work is all about.

@MEBYDESIGNTV:
Can you describe one thing that's critical to reaching your financial goals?

@MARTYNBULLARD:
You know, as an interior designer, we can work with budgets with millions and millions of dollars of other people's money. But when you have a

Below: Interior design by Martyn Lawrence Bullard. Photo by Douglas Friedman

company and it grows and you have all of your staff and your overhead and your building and all of those things that go into really creating and making a real brand, you've got to make sure that you've got the money to float that. So as much money as you have coming in, you know you're only making a very small portion of that. It can be hard to understand how to balance it all out, and an accountant is so important. You really need to make sure you understand your projections.

You need to make sure that you don't grow faster than your business will allow, than your clients that are coming in will allow. I'll look at my projects at the beginning of each year and say, what are my projects for this entire year? What's left from last year? What's new from this year? What are we expecting or hoping to come in? From doing that, we can come up with a rough estimate of what profit will come into the company, and from that, does it cover my overhead? If it doesn't cover your overhead, then you've got to reconfigure a little bit. If it does cover your overhead and there's more left over, then you work out, well, how do I grow? Do I start advertising more?

Every time we've had extra money, we developed a new product. So we keep enlarging the business in that way, so we'll add on a new furniture collection, or we'll come up with a new fabric collection, or now I'm doing things like jewelry. I have a beautiful, high-end jewelry collection about to launch. I've also got a fashion line coming out. So you know we've really taken this and expanded it into all the things that I love, but done it very carefully and making sure that we've monitored all of the money, all the finances, and kind of growing it, slowly but surely.

@MEBYDESIGNTV:
How do you define luxury?

@MARTYNBULLARD:
You know for me, the definition of luxury is really comfort. In today's crazy world where we've got the kind of media swirling and "Twittering" and "Instagramming" and all the madness, I believe that our homes really are our sanctuary, and that means a home has to be comfortable. You have to have great furniture that you can sit on, comfortable beds. I don't

want to have things around me that you can't touch because they're too precious. I really believe the ultimate word for today that really equals luxury is comfort.

@MEBYDESIGNTV:
How would you describe the essence of your brand?

@MARTYNBULLARD:
You know, it's very interesting because people always say to me, oh my god, you're more than an interior designer, you are a brand. And I've actually worked quite hard at that. I mean, I design eleven lines and work hand in hand with some of the most famous brands in the world, and those partnerships have become very special to me and have really turned my business into this brand. So, I believe that interior design today is not just about creating beautiful homes for your clients, it's really about learning how to expand and how to take that out into the world.

TV for me has been a big medium. Obviously I have TV shows playing at the moment in sixty countries around the world, so with 25 to 35 million people a week watching me on TV, some of those people are going to buy some of the stuff that I've been designing! And that's amazing, it's amazing to know other people want to have something that you've designed in their homes or in their offices or somehow in their life. That to me is the pinnacle of my career. I love that.

@MEBYDESIGNTV:
What are they buying emotionally?

@MARTYNBULLARD:
When people are buying my products, I feel like they want to have a little bit of my style, maybe a little bit of the style that they've seen I've developed for other clients. So, really and truly it's all about the idea of buying into what I do and buying into what I create. Some people may love what I've done for Cher's house or some people may love what I've done for Tommy Hilfiger's house. Those are two completely different styles, utterly, utterly different, but within that, there is still a core value

to the way I do things and the way I design things and that can be seen in my product.

So whether it's somebody that wants to have something because they want to feel like they're living like Cher, or whether it's somebody that just loves it because it's intrinsically beautiful, or they love the colors or they love the look of my fabric, or they love the way their food looks on the plates I've designed, I think it's all about an emotional response.

So how do you differentiate yourself in the marketplace?

We don't have a look. I don't have a specific thing where everything looks like a Mediterranean villa or I always use the color blue. That is so not what we're about. What we're about is creating completely customized, completely couture, if you like, interiors for my clients. I don't want you to walk into a client's home and go, "Martyn Lawrence Bullard did this." Whether the client says, "I want to live like an Indian princess, build me a Maharaja's palace," or if they want to feel like they're in Studio 54 every day, it's all about finding that dream and really becoming the purveyor of that dream.

To watch on-camera interviews with @MartynBullard visit www.youtube. com/mebydesigntv. Follow Martyn Lawrence Bullard on Instagram and Twitter @MartynBullard, on Pinterest @MartynLBullard, and on Facebook. com/MartynLawrenceBullard.

Why Not?

You did it! If you completed every STYLESheet™ in this book and answered the questions authentically, you've learned a lot about your business and how you can take it to the next level. I hope in these pages, you have found a new way of serving the world with your design talent at an even higher level. I also hope that the way you shape your business going forward keeps you aligned with the highest vision you have for yourself and your brand. Set a timeline for how long you'll take to implement the changes and then put one foot in front of the other and go.

I'm a big fan of why not? Why not send a letter to that celebrity whose home you have ideas for? Or the boutique hotel CEO whose properties you've always wanted to reinvent? The good news is that in the online world, people who were formerly off limits are just a tweet or a Facebook post away. Why not set your sights on the projects you've always dreamed of? You've got nothing to lose.

It's going to mean that sometimes you won't be sure, and sometimes you'll be afraid. But commit to stretch, dare, and be available. Growth is for designers who are committed to leadership. Let go of the resistance that comes when you're convinced that what you know is all there is. There is wisdom in innocence, power in being present. I think it's safe to say that you have no idea what could happen tomorrow, none. Or how your life and business could change in an instant. Will you make mistakes? Probably. Will opportunities you couldn't possibly anticipate show up along the way? I hope so! Go you!

About the Author

Kim Kuhteubl is an award-winning producer, writer, and member of the Producer's Guild Of America. She has packaged stories about interior design, real estate, and development in print, for television, and on digital platforms since 1999. As a filmmaker, her work has screened nationally and internationally in Africa, Europe, the Middle East, and the country where she was born, Canada. In 2011, she founded MeByDesign, an idea boutique for the design industry. MeByDesign boosts the brand value, visibility, and audience engagement of boutique interior design firms and legacy to-the-trade brands with a range of cross-platform, data-driven tools including digital storytelling, influencer and social media marketing, and bespoke video. The company also consults with executives and their teams on leadership and personal branding. Follow MeByDesign on Instagram or Twitter @mebydesigntv or on Facebook.com/mebydesign.

Acknowledgments

Thank you to the women I never knew whose whispers found their way into my research, some of whom I did not mention, and to those I do know, my clients who have trusted me with their journeys, colleagues, and my friends and teachers who have supported me along the way.

Elsie de Wolfe
Julia Morgan
Esther Pariseau
Lilian Rice
Sophia Hayden Bennett
Rose Cumming
Sara Holmes Boutelle
Ruby Ross Good
Frances Elkins
Marion Mahony Griffin
Norma Merrick Sklarek
Hutton Wilkinson
Margaret J. Anderson
Margaret Schiffer
Zaha Hadid
Hildegard Kuhteubl
Gina DeVee
Tracy Campoli
Catherine Collautt
Shawna Armstrong
Andrea Shields Nunez

Endnotes

Chapter Head Quotes

Chapter 1. Cherie Fehrman and Dr. Kenneth R. Fehrman, *Interior Design Innovators 1910–1960* (San Francisco: Fehrman Books, 2009),11.

Chapter 2. Kelly Hoppen in a video interview with the author, May 11, 2015.

Chapter 3. Dorothy Draper, *Decorating Is Fun!* (Garden City, N.Y.: Doubleday, 1962), 5–6.

Chapter 4. Billy Baldwin, *Billy Baldwin Decorates* (New Jersey: Chartwell Books, 1972), 9.

Chapter 5. David Netto, "The Decorator's Decorator," http://www.wsj.com/articles/SB10001424052748704380504575530334091983298 WSJ.com (October 9, 2010).

Chapter 6. Mario Buatta in a video interview with the author August 5, 2014.

Chapter 7. Barbara Barry in written interview obtained by the author, September 24, 2015.

Chapter 8. Clodagh in video interview with the author August 4, 2014.

Chapter 1

1. Cherie Fehrman and Dr. Kenneth R. Fehrman, *Interior Design Innovators 1910–1960* (San Francisco: Fehrman Books, 2009), 6.

2. Nina Campbell, *Elsie de Wolfe: A Decorative Life* (Clarkson Potter; 1st edition, 1992).

3. Peter Cohan, "Home Goods Ebiz Wayfair's 32% Growth Snags $165M Series A," Forbes.com (October 10, 2012). The US home goods market is $500 billion. The online portion represents six percent of that, or $30 billion, and is growing at a rate between 10 percent and 15 percent per year.

4. Wikipedia, s.v "List of Recessions in the United States," last modified January 9, 2016. https://en.wikipedia.org/wiki/List_of_recessions_in_the_United_States.

5. According to the Bureau of Labor Statistics, overall 23.2 percent of interior designers left the industry between 2008 and 2011.

6. Richard Morgan, "A Millionaire On Nearly Every Block in US: Study" NYPost.com (June 11, 2014).

7. Pew Research Center, "Executive Summary" in *Millennials: A Portrait Of Generation Next* (PewSocialTrends.org, February 24, 2010).

8. Ibid.

9. Frank, Betsy, Martin, Barry, Marci, Carl D., Rule, Randall, Hardy Williams, *A (Biometric) Day in the Life Emily* (Innerscope Research & Time Inc., April 2012), 3.

10. ComScore, "Next Generation Strategies for Advertising to Millennials (ComScore.com, January 24, 2012).

11. Shea Bennett, "How Do People Spend Their Time Online?" http://www.adweek.com/socialtimes/online-time/463670 (Adweek.com, May 7, 2012).

12. National Women's Business Council, "Why Invest In Women Fact Sheet" (NWBC.gov).

13. Mihaly Csikszentmihalyi, Creativity: *The Work and Lives of 91 Eminent People* (Harper Collins, 1996).

14. Daniel Pink, *A Whole New Mind: Why Right-brainers Will Rule the Future* (Riverhead Books, 2006).

15. Arlene Hirst, "Women In Design: Confronting The Glass Ceiling," http://www.interiordesign.net/articles/7894-women-in-design-confronting-the-glass-ceiling/ (InteriorDesign.net, September 11, 2013).

16. Liz McQuiston, *Women in Design: A Contemporary View* (Rizzoli International Publications, 1988), 7.

17. Women also place a higher value on innovation than men do. Some sixty-one percent of women consider this trait to be absolutely essential in a leader, compared with fifty-one percent of men. Pew Research Center. Chapter 2: "What Makes A Good Leader, and Does Gender Matter?" (PewSocialTrends.org, January 14, 2015).

18. Ibid.

Chapter 2

1. Jamie Adler CEO Phyllis Morris in discussion with the author, May 2014.

2. Simon Sinek, "Simon Sinek: How great leaders inspire action" (video file). Retrieved from https://www.ted.com/talks/simon_sinek_how_great_leaders_inspire_action?language=en, 2009.

3. George Avalos, "Report: Apple widens share of PC market despite slowing Mac sales," http://www.siliconbeat.com/2015/10/09/report-apple-widens-share-of-pc-market-despite-slowing-mac-sales/, October 9, 2105.

4. Compiled from her articles in newspapers and magazines and first published in 1914, de Wolf's book, *The House in Good Taste*, was ghost-written by Ruby Ross Wood. The edition referenced in this book was published by Rizzoli, 2004, with an introduction by Albert Hadley. Nina Campbell, *Elsie de Wolfe: A Decorative Life* (Clarkson Potter; 1st ed., 1992) 224.

5. Cherie Fehrman and Dr. Kenneth R. Fehrman, *Interior Design Innovators 1910–1960* (San Francisco: Fehrman Books, 2009), 6.

6. Apple Parish Bartlett and Susan Bartlett Crater, *Sister: The Life of Legendary American Interior Decorator Mrs. Henry Parish II* (St. Martin's Press, 2000).

7. Ibid.

8. Cherie Fehrman and Dr. Kenneth R. Fehrman, *Interior Design Innovators 1910–1960* (San Francisco: Fehrman Books, 2009), 10.

9. Albin Krebs, "Billy Baldwin is Dead at 80," *New York Times* (November 26, 1983).

10. Christopher Petkanas, "Ruby It's You," *New York Times* (March 30, 2010).

11. Ibid.

12. Ruby Ross Wood in collaboration with Rayne Adams, *The Honest House* (Forgotten Books, 2012, originally published 1914), 146.

13. Wikipedia, s.v "The Beverly Hills Hotel," https://en.wikipedia.org/wiki/The_Beverly_Hills_Hotel, last modified February 21, 2016.

14. Cherie Fehrman and Dr. Kenneth R. Fehrman, *Interior Design Innovators 1910–1960* (San Francisco: Fehrman Books, 2009), 24.

15. Ibid., 25.

16. Ibid., 25.

17. Ibid., 25.

18. Ibid., 25.

Chapter 3

1. Susan Jeffers, *Feel the Fear and Do It Anyway* (Ballantine Books, 20th anniversary edition, 2006).

2. Cherie Fehrman and Dr. Kenneth R. Fehrman, *Interior Design Innovators 1910–1960* (San Francisco: Fehrman Books, 2009), 11.

3. Ibid., 65.

4. Ibid., 66.

5. Ibid., 67–68.

6. Ibid., 53.

7. Source: www.knoll.com.

8. "Are Dyslexia and Wealth Linked? Study Finds Individuals With Dyslexia more likely to be millionaires." http://www.ldonline.org/article/5665/, 2003.

9. Kay Steiger, "When Women Don't Take Credit For Their Own Good Work," http://www.theatlantic.com/sexes/archive/2013/06/when-women-dont-take-credit-for-their-own-good-work/276555/, TheAtlantic.com, June 5, 2015.

10. Deborah Tannen William, *You Just Don't Understand: Women and Men in Conversation* (Morrow Paperbacks, 2007).

11. Sara Holmes Boutelle, *Julia Morgan Architect* (Abbeville Press: New York 1995), 169.

12. Ibid., 87.

13. "Women-Owned Businesses Key Facts, " WomanOwned.com, December 21, 2011.

14. A study from the University of Chicago discovered that men are ninety-four percent more likely than women to apply for a job where salary potential is dependent on outperforming their colleagues, as referenced in: Katherine Crowley and Kathi Elster, "Men vs. women: Why the work divide matters," http://upstart.bizjournals.com/resources/author/2013/01/10/male-versus-female-behavior-at-work.html?page=all, January 10, 2013.

15. Deborah Tannen William, *You Just Don't Understand: Women and Men in Conversation* (Morrow Paperbacks, 2007).

16. Sara Holmes Boutelle, *Julia Morgan Architect*, (Abbeville Press: New York, 1995), 17

17. Lamar Anderson, "How Women Are Climbing Architecture's Career Ladder," Curbed.com, March 17, 2014.

18. Jonathan Glancey, "I don't do nice," (TheGuardian.com, October 9th, 2006).

19. Sheena McKenzie, "Zaha Hadid: 'Would they still call me a diva if I was a man?'", CNN.com, August 21, 2014.

20. Donna Karan, "The 2010 Time 100: Zaha Hadid," *Time*, April 29, 2010.

21. Ibid.

22. Sheena McKenzie, "Zaha Hadid: 'Would they still call me a diva if I was a man?'", CNN.com, August 21, 2014.

Chapter 4

1. Wikipedia, sv "The Customer Is Always Right," https://en.wikipedia.org/wiki/The_customer_is_always_right, last modified August 3, 2015.

2. Bellaïche, Jean-Marc, Mei-Pochtler, Antonella, Hanisch Dorit, "The New World Of Luxury," (Boston Consulting Group, December 2010).

3. Dorothy Draper, *Decorating Is Fun!: How to be Your Own Decorator* was first published in 1939 on the eve of WWII.

4. Shawn Tully, Melanie Shanley and Joan Levinstein, "Taxpayer, Beware! Washington will soon be taking back a good chunk of that new tax cut. How? By using the sneakiest trap it's got: the Alternative Minimum Tax," *Fortune Magazine*, June 23, 2013.

5. Shawn Tully with Joan Caplin, "Look who pays for the bailout," *Fortune Magazine*, October 27, 2008.

Chapter 5

1. "Global internet users to reach 7.6 billion within the next 5 years," http://www.broadbandchoices.co.uk/news/2014/09/global-internet-users-230914, September 23, 2014.

2. Nicole Spector, "7 Keys To Creating A Brand Logo That Works Absolutely Everywhere," http://www.adweek.com/news/advertising-branding/7-keys-

creating-brand-logo-absolutely-works everywhere-168070, Adweek.com, November 11, 2015.

3. Denise Lee Yohn, "The Death Of The Tagline," http://www.adweek.com/news/advertising-branding/death-tagline-152255, Adweek.com, September 9, 2013.

4. Debbie, (a past client) in discussion with the author, Spring 2013.

5. "How Loading Time Affects Your Bottom Line," https://blog.kissmetrics.com/loading-time/.

6. Danny Wong, "In Q4, Social Media Drove 31.24% of Overall Traffic to Sites, Shareaholic Reports, Social Media, https://blog.shareaholic.com/social-media-traffic-trends-01-2015/, Shareaholic.com, Jan 26, 2015.

7. American Express, "Social Media Raises The Stakes For Customer Service," http://about.americanexpress.com/news/pr/2012/gcsb.aspx, Americanexpress.com, May 2, 2012.

8. Sergey Edunov, Carlos Diuk, Ismail Onur Filiz, Smriti Bhagat, and Moira Burke, "Three and a half degrees of separation," https://research.facebook.com/blog/three-and-a-half-degrees-of-separation/, Research.Facebook.com, February 4, 2016.

9. Ash Read, "11 Facebook Tips, Tricks and Facts You Probably Don't Already know," https://blog.bufferapp.com/facebook-tips, Blog.bufferapp.com, February 15, 2016.

10. "Marketing Benchmarks From 7,000+ Businesses," http://cdn1.hubspot.com/hub/53/Marketing-Benchmarks-from-7000-businesses.pdf.

11. Ash Read, "11 Facebook Tips, Tricks and Facts You Probably Don't Already know," https://blog.bufferapp.com/facebook-tips, Blog.bufferapp.com, February 15, 2016.

12. Maeve Duggan, Nicole B. Ellison, Cliff Lampe, Amanda Lenhart, and Mary Madden, "Demograhics of Key Social Networking Platforms," http://www.pewinternet.org/2015/01/09/demographics-of-key-socialnetworking-platforms-2/, Pew Research Center, January 9, 2015.

Chapter 6

1. ElleDecor.com.

2. Susan Orlean, "This Is Perfect," *New Yorker,* April 19, 1994.

Chapter 7

1. Jillian D'Onfor, "Pinterest Says More Guys Are Joining The Site Than Ever. Here's What They're Doing," Business Insider, March 31, 2015.

2. InternetRetailer.com.

3. "45 Video Marketing Statistics," http://www.virtuets.com/45-video-marketing-statistics/.

4. Statistic Brain Research Institute, "Walmart Company Statistics," http://www.statisticbrain.com/Walmart-company-statistics/, January 25, 2016.
5. YouTube.com.
6. "Small Businesses Are So-So About Social," emarketer.com, April 14, 2015.
7. Natalie Jarvey, "New Fronts: YouTube Emphasizes Engagement With Help From Grace Helbig, John Green," *Hollywood Reporter*, April 29, 2015.
8. Robin Klehr Avia (regional managing principal and chair of the board at Gensler), in discussion with the author, 2014.
9. Fred Schmidt, Global Corporate Interiors Practice chair at Perkins+Will, in discussion with the author, 2014.

Chapter 8

1. Kickstarter.com.
2. https://www.kickstarter.com/projects/fossflakes/danish-sleep-pillow-design-comfort-inspired-by-sno-0?ref=nav_search.
3. Licensing Expo 2012.
4. Ellie Altshuler (Nixon Peabody), in discussion with the author, May 2014.
5. Vanessa Friedman and Jacob Bernstein, "Donna Karan Steps Down In Major Shift For Fashion," *New York Times*, June 30, 2015.
6. https://www.ftc.gov/tips-advice/business-center/advertising-and-marketing.
7. Betty Kelly Sargent, "Surprising Self-Publishing Statistics," *Publisher's Weekly*, July 28, 2014.
8. Tony Ash, "Copyists Are Eating Away At The Creativity Of Our Industry," http://www.dezeen.com/2015/01/08/tony-ash-md-vitra-copyists-creativity-design-industry-intellectual-property/, Dezeen.com, January 8, 2015.
9. US Department Of State, Freedom Of Information Act, "The Privacy Act," https://foia.state.gov/Learn/PrivacyAct.aspx.
10. CreativeCommons.Org.
11. http://www.copyright.gov/legislation/dmca.pdf.

Resources

1. Website Templates & Tools

Most personal brand websites are built in Wordpress, but many creative types use Square Space, too.

- Competethemes.com (free blog templates in Wordpress)
- ElegantThemes.com
- Google Keyword Tool: https://adwords.google.com/KeywordPlanner (Use this to help you figure out terms for SEO.)
- Shopify.com (out-of-the-box e-commerce solutions to build your online store)
- SquareSpace.com
- StudioPressThemes.com
- ThemeForest.com
- Tumblr.com
- WooCommerce.com
- Wordpress plugin: SEO by Yoast

2. Set Up Your Newsletter

Use any of these email marketing service providers to set up and distribute your newsletter. I love mailchimp.com, which is free until you reach 2,000 subscribers.

- AWeber.com
- ConstantContact.com
- Mailchimp.com

3. Get Listed

The point of having an online home is to invite your unique audience to it and then compel them to buy your services or at least sign up for your newsletter.

Make sure you've registered your site at google.com/analytics and that your developer or virtual assistant has added the tracking code so you can see who is visiting, from where, and how long they're staying.

Google (google.com/addurl/)

Association Of Interior Designers (ASID.org, *If you qualify for membership.*)

IIDA.org

Houzz.com

Yelp.com

Zillow.com

International Federation Of Interior Architects & Designers (ifiworld.org)

HGTV Professionals Network http://people.hgtv.com/professionals/

4. List Your Inventory Here

You will use a combination of online marketing, trade and licensing shows, and salespeople to market your collection. One of the best ways to drive traffic to your site is to list your products with an existing marketplace and capitalize on their marketing efforts. Here are a few good ones:

- 1stdibs.com (collectibles and antiques. Ask about their trade program.)
- Chairish.com (Ask about their trade program.)
- Etsy.com (Anything goes if it's handmade; don't be fooled, there are a lot of high-priced items on the site now, too.)
- Viyet.com (Ask about their trade program.)

5. Social Media Tools & Apps

- Buffer.com (Pinterest, Twitter, Facebook, LinkedIn, Google+)
- Hootsuite.com (Twitter, Facebook, LinkedIn, Google+, Wordpress)
- Iconosquare (Key metrics about your instagram account)
- Instacollage (Create collages with Instagram. Download from the App store.)
- Latergram.me (Instagram)
- Studio (Instagram. Download from the App store.)
- Unfollow (Twitter. Download from the App store.)
- Watermark (Download from the App store.)

6. Product Crowdsourcing

- Indiegogo.com
- Kickstarter.com
- Quirky.com (The submission projects help you build a comprehensive virtual invention. You can do these by yourself or teamwork-style with other community members.)

7. Get On TV

Your favorite show might be looking for guests. Here are a couple of casting resources.

- DIY: http://www.diynetwork.com/about-us/be-on-diy
- HGTV: http://www.hgtv.com/shows/be-on-hgtv
- www.interiordesignercasting.com (Design show casting accessed by production companies and studio executives)
- http://www.tlc.com/tv-shows/other-shows/about-our-shows/tlc-casting/

8. Legalese

- www.creativecommons.org
- Copyscape.com (A free plagiarism checker for finding copies of your web pages online)
- http://www.termsfeed.com (Terms and Conditions generator)
- Ithenticate.com
- http://www.uspto.gov/trademarks-application-process/filing-online

9. Books

- *A Whole New Mind*, by David Pink
- *Big Magic*, by Elizabeth Gilbert
- *Feel the Fear and Do It Anyway*, by Susan Jeffers
- *Playing Big*, by Tara Sophia Mohr
- *Smart Women Finish Rich*, by David Bach